# a fresh look at fish

# a fresh look at fish

SONIA STEVENSON

MITCHELL BEAZLEY

# Dedication

*This book is dedicated to Percy O'Donnell, friend for 30 years and fishmonger for 25 of them, who in that time taught me all I now know about fish.*

Sonia Stevenson *A Fresh look at Fish*

First published in Great Britain in 1996 by Mitchell Beazley,
an imprint of Reed International Books Limited,
Michelin House, 81 Fulham Road, London SW3 6RB
and Auckland, Melbourne, Singapore and Toronto.

ISBN 185732 8620

A CIP record catalogue is available from the British Library.

Produced by Mandarin Offset
Printed in China

Editor: Lewis Esson
Designer: Fiona Knowles
Commissioning Editor: Sue Jamieson
Executive Art Editor: Fiona Knowles
Jacket design: Fiona Knowles
Photography: Jeremy Hopley, assisted by Catherine Rowlands
Home Economist: Annie Nichols
Stylist: Wei Tang
Production Controller: Christina Quigley
Indexer: Hilary Bird

Mitchell Beazley thanks Formica for supplying the backgrounds for photography.

---

Notes

All recipes serve 6 unless otherwise stated.

Both metric and imperial measurements have been given in all recipes. Use one set of measurements and not a mixture of both.

Standard level spoon measurements are used in all recipes.
      1 tablespoon = one 15ml spoon
      1 teaspoon = one 5ml spoon

Eggs should be size 3 unless otherwise stated.
Milk should be full fat unless otherwise stated.

Fresh herbs should be used unless otherwise stated. If unavailable use dried herbs as an alternative but halve the quantities stated.

Ovens should be preheated to the specified temperature – if using a fan-assisted oven, follow the manufacturer's instructions for adjusting time and temperature.

# contents

# foreword

The welcome idea in *A Fresh Look at Fish* is that of adapting each of the wonderful recipes to a range of fish that will work equally well cooked the same way. So often people feel that they can't cook a particularly exciting dish because they can't get the right fish for it.

A book of fish cookery from Sonia Stevenson is a great excitement to me. No one had greater influence than Sonia on my development from a mere seafood bar type of a cook to something a lot more ambitious. During the 70s and 80s the Horn of Plenty at Gulworthy near Tavistock was the most perfect restaurant for us. Sonia and her husband Patrick had such stylish ideas and the cooking was outstanding, particularly the fish cookery. Her dishes of thick fillets of sea bass with beautifully light and exquisitely flavoured butter sauces I will never forget. Her lobster quenelles are still on our menu at The Seafood Restaurant, as is her baked hake with lemon, onion and butter.

Sonia's particular strength is in her deep knowledge of sauces which are used throughout this book, making it essential reading for anyone who wants to cook fish in a Northern European style.

*Rick Stein*

7

# introduction

With so many varieties and such a difference in sizes it is small wonder that choosing a recipe for a fish dish becomes totally bewildering. We are spoilt for choice, but by looking at the problem another way life immediately becomes a great deal simpler. Fish, after all, are just meat, skin and bones and they can be divided very conveniently into categories according to their shape. Recipes can similarly be divided into these groups, and the choice of fish used then becomes arbitrary – simply choose according to what looks best in the fishmonger that day, how much money you want to spend or the occasion.

This book is written with such an approach in mind. The recipes are grouped into sections and apply to shapes of fish rather than named individuals. Suggestions of the fish you might like to work with are listed in a column at the side of the recipe. Many of the recipes here will work with all kinds of fish and indeed one recipe used again and again with a different fish will probably be so different in flavour that there's a possibility your family or friends won't even recognise it!

Using this approach you don't even need to feel lost when you see a fish you have never come across before. Look at its shape and ask some questions. Is it round, or flat, or does it have a shell? Has it lots of scales which are better removed before you start cooking? Or none? The book aims to answer all these sorts of questions, and help overcome the stumbling block of thinking that you have to know all about fish before you cook it.

It is true that every fresh fish has its own identifiable flavour, and I say 'fresh' advisably, for the more stale a fish becomes the

8

less individual its flavour is. Fish are not hung like meat as there is no need to tenderize them although some people think that the best flavour is achieved from a Dover sole after it has rested a few days and got rid of the uric acid in its flesh as it is excreted through its skin. But then they also say this about skate and in my opinion this is totally untrue - the older the skate the nastier it becomes, and the fresher it is the better.

Usually the more expensive the fish, the more delicious the flavour, which is why Dover soles make a dinner party dish and dabs a homely one. But at the same time, really fresh dabs are infinitely preferable to old smelly sole and with a little bit of extra effort can be transformed for a dinner!

A word of warning: the wonderful flexibility of fish falls down when it comes to cooking time in that overcooking any fish will ruin the dish. Having said that the aim of this book is to reveal how easy fish cookery can be, and how often a wide variety of fish will suit this or that recipe.

Madame Prunier says in the foreword to her *Fish Cookery Book* 'that it deals with those (species) that are – so erroneously – known as common. I firmly believe that all fish are equally good if they reach the table fresh, well cooked and tastefully served...'

Well so do I!

*Sonia Stevenson*

9

# flat fish & fillets

Flat fish are a boon to the fish cook and seem almost purpose-built for the kitchen as their slim build and simple bone structure mean that they cook fast and evenly, and flesh and bones are easily separated

## TYPES OF FLAT FISH

Of the fish in this section, the big flat fish are halibut, turbot and brill; the smaller ones include plaice (usually), the soles, flounders and dab. Did you know that plaice can rival the turbot for size? About 90cm (3ft) is their maximum, but that's rare, whereas for a turbot 1m is much more common.

Other fish, such as John Dory, bream, mullet, snapper and pomfret are included in this section because they cook like flat fish, although they are technically round fish (see pages 56-9) – with their eyes in the normal position – but flat in effect. Skate wings are also included in this section because of their cooking qualities.

## FLAT FISH FILLETS

Flat fish are often used in a filleted form, either for deep-frying or presenting rolled up. Get your fishmonger to do the filleting for you, but be sure to ask for the bones and skin to make a stock.

When preparing fillets for poaching and presenting flat, I find the best way is to poach the whole fish in a stock, then slip the fillets off the bone and use them as they are. You still have the stock they were cooked in to make your sauce, and the texture of the flesh will be much better because the flesh remains stretched as it is cooked – and the result is a much juicier piece, which also weighs more as there is less water loss.

Skate is, in my opinion, best filleted before cooking because the open structure of the flesh (which tends to fall apart if filleted later) can contract and tighten into a neat, firm portion of fish. It is not usually sold as a whole fish, only as 'wings' and is the same part as the frill around a turbot, only much extended. It has a cartilaginous framework – no bones but equally infuriating.

Also included in this section are the fillets of round fish; the larger ones are sliced to the size you need, but the smaller ones can be used as they are.

An interesting little item of knowledge to help you choose your flat fish fillets – the brown

BRILL – *Left-handed fish, along with turbot and megrim, but flavour inferior. Good texture. Often cooked whole. Average size about 30cm/1ft: max. 60cm/2ft. No scales. Upper price range.*

DAB – *Small fish with watery flesh and average-to-poor flavour. OK when very fresh. Usually sold filleted. Readily available. No scales. Very cheap.*

DOVER SOLE – *Medium-sized fish, with close-textured flesh and excellent flavour. Available in all sizes. Small scales. Usually skinned both sides and grilled whole or filleted. Small ones called 'slip' soles. Expensive.*

FLOUNDER – *Inferior to plaice in flavour, with slightly watery flesh. Some scales. Generally cheap.*

GREENLAND HALIBUT – *Similar to halibut, but inferior flavour and watery flesh. No scales. Usually sold in fillets. Medium price range.*

HALIBUT – *Biggest right-handed flat fish, up to 2m/7ft. Firm white flesh, but it can be dry. Excellent served cold. Whole small fish, called 'chicken halibut', available from 1kg/2¼ lb. No scales. Medium to expensive price range. Do not confuse with inferior 'Greenland' variety.*

side is best as it is always the thickest and meatiest (being the top of the fish).

## COOKING WHOLE FISH

I know that cooking a fish whole can present problems through its sheer size. Just try handling a whole halibut, turbot (or tuna!). Very few people have a *turbotière,* the enormous round fish kettle designed to poach the turbot whole. A full-sized halibut is too large even for such an enormous cooking vessel, as they can grow to 2m (7ft) long. Fish of this size are always sold in cutlets, in which case you can apply any round fish recipe to it. The same is true for turbot, tuna, swordfish and any of the other giants.

Smaller specimens can be wrapped in foil with some stock and herbs, giving an excellent imitation of a fish kettle – or even an improvement on it, as all the juices are kept in.

Whole fish usually have to be skinned after cooking, otherwise the flesh rips away with it. However, Dover soles are an exception and are a positive pleasure to skin raw. There is a knack to it: the skin is pulled off at an angle from just above the eyes to diagonally opposite under the tail, or vice versa, leaving a white web of fibres covering the flesh that holds it firmly together. Skate is the other exception to skinning – leave it to the professionals, unless you are very muscular or need some sandpaper!

Sometimes, as with turbot, you may want to eat the skin, so you just leave it on. However, if the fish has large, inedible scales, you should remove them. This problem I have dealt with in the introduction to round fish (see pages 56-9), as it is mostly among this group that they are found. Otherwise, scales tend to be light, often invisible, and edible.

Remember that denser fish, such as turbot, will take longer to cook than open-textured ones like brill. As we are dealing here with thin portions rather than cutlets the problem hardly affects us, it is again much more a matter for the round fish section.

JOHN DORY – *(Technically a round fish but included here as it is so flat.) Use scissors to trim off any bony protuberances. Excellent texture and flavour, but tough skin. No scales. Upper price range due to the small proportion of flesh to bone.*

MEGRIM – *Same family as brill and turbot. Light scales. Medium quality, middle price range.*

PLAICE – *Medium to large fish, with a beautiful flavour when fresh. Bad buy in February/March, when spawning. Available whole or filleted. No scales. Middle price range.*

SKATE – *Only sold as 'wings', which can be very large and are used as flat fish. Many-sectioned gelatinous frame and rough, inedible skin. Excellent flavour when in good condition. Can have unpleasant ammonia smell when old – or sometimes just by chance – that does not improve with cooking. Medium to expensive.*

TURBOT – *Large fish, white and firm-fleshed, with fabulous flavour. Sold in cutlets and fillets. Smaller 'chicken' turbot sold whole. No scales. Makes excellent stock. Usually obtainable from larger suppliers. Very expensive.*

WITCH OR 'TORBAY' SOLE – *Average-size fish with average flavour. Flesh a little watery, but firm. Readily available. Middle price range.*

# Steaming Whole Fish

OPTIONS
*Brill, chicken turbot,
John Dory, mackerel, plaice,
salmon, sea bass, sole, trout*

6 whole fish,
each weighing about
450g/1lb, trimmed

2 stalks of lemon grass,
sliced in half, or small bunch
of fresh herbs, such as tarragon,
red fennel, lemon balm
or dill (optional)

salt and freshly ground black pepper

115g/4oz slightly salted butter,
melted and acidulated
with lemon juice,
sauce beurre blanc (page 185)
or cold crème fraîche,
to serve

*The best ways to steam fish are either to roll it in wet paper and then bake it in the oven or simply cover it and cook in the microwave. This latter is an excellent means when just cooking for two people, but having to cook fish only two at a time means that it takes too long when serving six. Wrapping each fish individually in wet paper, then baking them all together and unrolling them only just before serving suits fish to a 't'. The skin usually comes off with the paper.*

*Served with an acidulated melted butter, a beurre blanc or crème fraîche, this is a very simple and delicious way to treat fish, provided the fish is really super-fresh.*

Wet 3–4 sheets of greaseproof paper thoroughly, wrap the seasoned fish in about 4 turns of it, adding fennel, lemon grass or fresh herbs alongside the fish if you want to perfume it. Then wrap in a couple of sheets of wet newspaper, 6 turns in all.

Cook as described above. Allow about 5 minutes for the heat to penetrate the paper, then give individual flat fish only 5 minutes more and round ones 10 minutes (flat fish take less time to cook than round fish).

# *Whole Roast Fish*

*As large whole fish always provide just the four fillets, when you lift the fillets off the bone to serve, for six people you need to cut one-third off each fillet and divide these off-cuts among the remaining two plates. Alternatively you can cut all the fillets into thirds and put two of these on each plate.*

Preheat the oven to 230°C/450°F/gas8.

In a small saucepan, simmer together the shallots with half the butter for 5 minutes. Add the mushrooms and lemon juice mixed with 1 tablespoon of water. Cook for 2 minutes. Add the remaining butter, the stock and the cream. Season lightly and bring to the boil.

Pour this into a large roasting dish, lay the fish on top and baste with the mixture. Cover completely with foil and bake in the oven for 30 minutes, or until the flesh can be eased away from the bones. Remove the fish from the dish, take off the dark skin and place the fish on a large serving dish.

Strain the juices into a small pan and reduce to about 300 ml/½ pint. Whisk in the hollandaise sauce base, adjust the seasoning if necessary and pour over the fish to serve.

OPTIONS
*Halibut, large plaice, turbot*

1 whole large flat fish, weighing about 1.75-2.25kg/4-5lb, trimmed

6 shallots, chopped

225g/8oz butter

175g/6oz mushrooms, sliced

1 teaspoon lemon juice

285g/10oz fish stock

50g/2oz double cream

150ml/¼ pint hollandaise sauce base (page 184)

salt and freshly ground black pepper

# Pan-grilled Whole Fish with Tomatoes

OPTIONS
*Skinned bream, small brill,
John Dory, plaice,
fillets of red mullet, whole sole*

6 whole flat fish, each weighing
about 350g/12oz, or 12 skinned
fillets, each weighing 50-85g/2-3oz

3 or 4 garlic cloves, chopped

about 150ml/¼ pint olive oil

85g/3oz fresh breadcrumbs

6 large tomatoes

1 tablespoon sugar

2 tablespoons chopped parsley

5 tablespoons red wine vinegar

1 tablespoon Pernod

salt and freshly ground black pepper

1 French loaf, to serve

*Question – is this dish just an excuse for cooking these delicious tomatoes? Well, they are marvellous together so don't even bother to answer! The Pernod at the end is for pepping up more humbly flavoured fish.*

Fry the garlic to a light brown in 3 tablespoons of the oil. Do not overcook or it will become bitter. Lift it out with a slotted spoon, letting it drain well.

Adding more oil if necessary, fry the breadcrumbs until golden and add them to the garlic.

Lightly oil a ridged grilling pan and heat it until very hot. Slice the tomatoes in half and lay them skin-side down on the ridges to mark them.

Turn them over into a hot frying-pan with 100ml/3½fl oz of the olive oil and sprinkle with the sugar and lots of black pepper. Now cook them over a high heat to let them concentrate their flavour without disturbing them and they will char and caramelize.

Sprinkle the garlic, breadcrumbs and chopped parsley over, season with salt and lift them into an ovenproof dish.

Brush the fish with oil and salt, dip in flour and place on the ridged grilling pan. After 4 minutes, turn the fish over and cook for a further 4 minutes.

In a small pan, boil the red wine vinegar down to about one-third of its volume. Add 1 tablespoon of the oil and the Pernod. Bring it to the boil.

Just before serving, reheat the tomatoes under the grill and baste the fish with the reduced vinegar mixture after you dish it up. Serve with crusty bread.

# Grilled Fish with Hazelnuts and Radicchio

*Grilled vegetables have become very popular lately. The radicchio in this recipe can be enhanced with some grilled asparagus tips. Alternatively you can replace the radicchio with heads of chicory, or even hearts of baby celery.*

Preheat the oven to 190°C/375°F/gas5.

Slice the radicchio in half through the root, wash if necessary and shake to drain. Now brush the pieces with some hazelnut oil and salt and place them under the grill. Turn them once and, when they have wilted and slightly charred, arrange them in a casserole with 3 tablespoons of water. Sprinkle with chopped black olives, the freshly toasted hazelnuts and the anchovy. Cook them in the oven for up to half an hour.

When the radicchio are almost cooked, preheat the grill well again, oil the rack underneath and heat it up also.

Oil the fish itself and rub salt and pepper over it. Dust it with flour if you like a slight crust on the outside. Place under the hot grill. Turn the fish after 3 or 4 minutes and grill the other side.

Slip the fish on to warmed plates and serve with the radicchio mixture.

OPTIONS
*Small brill, Dover sole, John Dory, lemon sole, plaice*

6 whole fish,
each weighing about
350g/12oz (skinned if they are
Dover sole)

3 heads of radicchio

hazelnut oil, for brushing

6 black olives, chopped

50g/2oz chopped hazelnuts, lightly toasted in a dry frying pan

6 anchovy fillets, cut into pieces

salt and freshly ground black pepper

flour for dusting (optional)

# Flat Fish en Papillote

OPTIONS
*Bream, John Dory, soles*

6 small whole flat fish,
head and fins removed and scaled

2 onions

175g/6oz butter

1 teaspoon dried thyme

freshly grated nutmeg to taste

1 teaspoon lemon juice

3 tablespoons mixed chopped
tarragon, parsley and chives

6 bay leaves

salt and freshly ground black pepper

*Should you wish to serve whole individual fish, it is difficult to find enough room under a grill to cook them all at once. Baking is simple, but tends to dry out the fish rather than give it a grilled effect. Paper bags do seem to fit the bill as they keep the fish moist but not sodden, and yet dry but not dried out. Cooking the fish over a mixture of red peppers, garlic and anchovies is another way of helping to keep it moist and it also adds flavour.*

Preheat the oven to 250°C/475°F/gas9.

Make a savoury base on which to lay the fish as follows: chop the onions finely and cook them in two-thirds of the butter until they soften, adding water as necessary to prevent them browning. When they are soft, season them with salt, thyme and several gratings of nutmeg and black pepper.

In another pan, melt the remaining butter, add the lemon juice and bring to the boil.

Cut 6 oblongs of baking parchment each about 5cm/2in larger than the fish all round when folded in half. Now spoon one-sixth of the onions on half of one of the oblongs and lay one of the fish on top.

Stir the mixed chopped herbs into the lemon butter and, using a pastry brush, coat the fish with it. Add a bay leaf and roll up the 3 edges of the paper to enclose the fish in an loose but airtight parcel. Repeat this for the other fish.

Bake the parcels in the oven for 10 to 15 minutes, by which time they should have puffed up and browned.

Place an empty plate in the centre of the table for the empty bags and serve the fish parcels unopened on individual plates.

# Packages of Fillets with Tomato & White Butter Sauce

*Because the fish steams in its own juice, cooking fish in foil seals in all the flavours and goodness. As the types of fish required for this dish are mostly those with a more delicate flavour, the quality of the fish used is even more important than usual.*

Preheat the oven to 200°C/400°F/gas6.

Boil together the white wine, onion, 30g/1oz of the butter, the garlic and some pepper until there are only about 3 tablespoons of liquid left. Top up with cold water to make 250ml/8fl oz.

Place the fillets in this liquid and leave to marinate for about 1 hour. Drain, reserving the marinade.

Arrange the herbs on 6 of the fillets, top with ½ a bay leaf, then place another fillet on top of each. Wrap the fish and herb 'sandwiches' together with 2 slices of bacon each. (Season the fish only if the bacon seems very unsalted.)

Lay each of the 'sandwiches' on one half of an oiled square of foil. Fold over the other half of the sheet and seal the edges by pleating or crimping to form loose but airtight parcels.

Bake in the oven for about 20 minutes (to judge when the fish is ready carefully press the outside; it should feel firm to the touch).

Towards the end of this time, add the rest of the butter and lemon juice to the marinade, with salt to taste. Boil it up until it emulsifies. Strain it into a sauce-boat and add the tiny tomato dice.

Transfer the fish parcels to warmed plates, half open them and serve the sauce separately.

OPTIONS
*Brill, chicken turbot,
Dover sole, John Dory*

12 skinned fish fillets,
each weighing about 85g/3oz

150ml/¼ pint white wine

1 onion, finely chopped

225g/8oz unsalted butter

1 garlic clove, chopped and crushed

12 basil leaves, torn

1½ tablespoons chopped parsley

3 teaspoons fresh thyme leaves,
picked over

3 bay leaves, halved

12 thin slices of streaky bacon
or prosciutto

juice of 1 lemon

2 tomatoes, peeled, deseeded and
cut into tiny dice

salt and freshly ground black pepper

grapeseed or groundnut oil,
for greasing

# White Wine Sauces

OPTIONS
*Any fish*

3 fish, each weighing 675g/1½lb
when trimmed of head and tail
1 tablespoon finely chopped shallots

25g/¾oz butter

300ml/½ pint white wine or Noilly
Prat white vermouth

450ml/¾ pint of fish stock
(page 183) or water

*for a flour-thickened sauce:*
30g/1oz flour

45g/1½oz butter

small triangles of pastry, to serve

2 tablespoons grated Cheddar
(optional)

*for a cream-and-egg-thickened sauce:*
150ml/¼ pint double cream

1 egg yolk

*A reduction of white wine with stock forms the base of many classic sauces. Add a roux and the result is the velouté family of sauces. Add cream to the velouté, and the result is sauce suprème; add egg yolks to that, and you get sauce normande. This is demonstrated by the Fish Sauce Family Tree on page 187.*

*The modern trend is to avoid adding flour to sauces. So leave it out and continue as above. The idea is the same, but produces a thinner and richer sauce.*

Preheat the oven to 180°C/350°F/gas4.

Simmer the shallots in the butter and wine or vermouth until there is only about 2 tablespoons. Add the fish stock or water and mix well. Season.

Place the fish in a large roasting tin and pour the wine mixture over, adding more water to cover if necessary. Put it in the oven and cook for 8-10 minutes, until the flesh will lift away from the bone.

If you don't care for the skins, scrape them off now, adding them together with any bones to the liquid.

Lift away the flesh from the bones in whole fillets and lay these either in one big warmed serving dish or divide them between 6 individual warmed plates.

Top up the liquid remaining in the baking tin with 300ml/½ pint of water and bring back to the boil on the top of the stove. Then strain it into a saucepan and reduce to about 300ml/½ pint.

Choose one of the following methods to thicken the sauce:
1. With flour and served plain or grilled with cheese: melt 30g/1oz of the butter in a saucepan and stir in the flour. Cook together without browning for about a minute. Over this mixture (known as a 'roux'), pour the hot fish stock and whisk over a high heat until boiling. Add the cream and simmer the sauce until it will coat the back of a spoon. Beat in the remaining butter and season. Pour over the fillets and serve with small triangles of pastry or sprinkle with the grated Cheddar cheese and brown under the grill.

2. Without flour: Add the double cream to the hot fish stock and thicken by boiling off one-third of the liquid, until the sauce lightly clings to the back of a spoon before dripping off. Season. Whisk together the egg yolk with 1 teaspoon water, preferably over heat or in a double-boiler, and fold into the sauce. Serve either poured over the fillets or browned under the grill.

# Paupiettes of Fish with Mushrooms and Cheese

*'Paupiettes' are fillets that are rolled up loosely and presented with the tail end making a nice 'V'. Any fillet will do, but the cooking time will vary a bit according to the density of the fish. Also, 50g/2oz of sole will fill you up to the same extent as 115g/4oz of whiting, because sole is all meat and fibre, whereas whiting has much more water content, which oozes out during the cooking. You can use one large fillet per person if you so wish.*

Slice the mushrooms thinly and fry them in the butter in a deep frying pan for 2 minutes. Season.

Add the lemon juice mixed with 5 tablespoons of water and a little salt. Boil up and set aside for 5 minutes. Then drain into a bowl, keeping some mushrooms for garnish.

Divide the rest between the fillets, which are then loosely folded around them, leaving the tail pieces showing for decoration. Brush with the mushroom juices, then put them in a frying pan. Cover and cook gently for 7 to 10 minutes, basting from time to time. Lift them out and keep warm.

Add the cheese to the pan and squash it with a wooden spoon, blending it with the juices, boiling down to a smooth, thick cream.

Now add the crème fraîche and re-heat, adding any extra juice from the waiting paupiettes.

Finally, place the paupiettes on warmed plates, pour the sauce over and pile the extra garnishing mushrooms on top with some coriander leaves.

OPTIONS
*Fillets of any fish*

12 fish fillets, each weighing about 85g/3oz

350g/12oz firm white button mushrooms

140g/5oz butter

3 teaspoons fresh lemon juice

85g/3oz Roquefort cheese

300ml/½ pint crème fraîche

few fresh coriander leaves, to garnish

# *Whole Flat Fish with Hazelnut Oil and Wild Mushrooms*

OPTIONS
*Brill, Dover sole (pictured), chicken turbot, John Dory, pomfret*

6 whole flat fish, each weighing about 450g/1lb

225g/8oz girolles or other wild mushrooms

5 tablespoons grapeseed or groundnut oil, plus more for brushing

5 tablespoons hazelnut oil

1 tablespoon nibbed hazelnuts

2 garlic cloves, chopped

2 teaspoons lemon juice mixed with 1 tablespoon water

2 tablespoons chopped parsley

salt and freshly ground black pepper

*You have to fillet flat fish in order to skin them raw, except for Dover sole; however, the flesh of fish has a better texture if it is cooked on the bone. Therefore, unwanted skin has to be peeled off after it has been cooked. Luckily, with some fish, eating the skin is an added bonus.*

Preheat the oven to 230°C/450°F/gas8 and heat a ridged grill pan. Brush both the pan and the fish with oil.

With a pair of scissors, trim away the outermost frill from the fish and also remove the head. Season the fish.

Grill the dark side of the fish for about 4 minutes. Turn the fish over on to a plate and then slide on to a lipped baking sheet. Repeat for all the remaining fish. Put the fish to cook in the oven for about 8 minutes.

Meanwhile, clean the mushrooms and rinse if necessary. Take a large pan and fry the nuts and garlic in the mixed oils until they begin to brown. Throw in the mushrooms and cook them lightly. Season and stir in the lemon juice and parsley.

Remove the skin from the cooked fish at this point if you wish, then lift them on to plates, pour the mushroom sauce over and serve.

# Paupiettes of Fish with Fromage Frais

OPTIONS
*Brill, chicken turbot, dab, plaice, soles, whiting*

12 small or 6 large skinned fillets of flat fish

115g/4oz butter

140g/5oz mushrooms, sliced

1 garlic clove, crushed

1 teaspoon lemon juice

225g/8oz fromage frais

2 tablespoons Dijon mustard

1 tablespoon chopped parsley

pinch of paprika

salt and freshly ground black pepper

*This kind of stuffing can be varied by using more strongly flavoured herbs like tarragon or basil instead of parsley. For a special occasion, use wild mushrooms.*

Preheat the oven to 200°C/400°F/gas6.

Melt half the butter in a frying pan and cook the mushrooms and garlic together for 2-3 minutes. Pour in the lemon juice mixed with about 2 tablespoons water and boil it away.

Turn the mushrooms into a bowl and mix in all the other ingredients except the remaining butter and the fish. Season well.

Fold or roll the fillets into paupiettes with some of the mushroom stuffing inside. Arrange them in an ovenproof dish and spoon any extra stuffing on top. Dot with the rest of the butter, cover with foil and bake for 15 to 20 minutes.

Serve with the juices poured over.

# Pan-fried Fish Fillets with Shallots, Garlic and Rosemary

*Shallots and onions must be well cooked to enjoy their sweet flavour to the full. To make sure that they do not brown in the initial cooking, add 2 or 3 tablespoons of water to the butter; this has the effect of cooking them by boiling them before they dry out and eventually sauté in the butter.*

In a frying pan, simmer the chopped onions in the butter with 2 or 3 tablespoons of water until the water has all evaporated and the onions are frying gently in the butter.

Add the garlic and herbs, followed by the fish fillets. Season well and allow the fish to cook gently in the mixture, about 5 minutes. Squeeze in lemon juice to taste.

Remove the rosemary and serve with the onion mixture piled on top of the fish. Spinach and new potatoes are good accompaniments.

OPTIONS

*Brill, chicken turbot, halibut, John Dory, plaice, sea bass, sole*

6 skinned fish fillets, each weighing 50-85g/2-3oz, or equivalent

225g/8oz onions, finely chopped

115g/4oz unsalted (or slightly salted) butter

1 garlic clove

1 teaspoon dried thyme

3 sprigs of fresh rosemary

juice of 1 lemon

salt and freshly ground black pepper

# Pan-fried Fish Fillets with Basil and Tomato

*Since this dish has an Italianate aura, the cooking medium should be an oil – perhaps an olive oil, but not necessarily very virgin unless you enjoy its strong taste.*

Heat half the oil in a large saucepan and add the garlic. Allow it to brown a little. Throw in the tomatoes, cook and pulp them down until they start to fry.

Add the wine and boil rapidly to reduce the liquid until the mixture begins to fry again and then add the basil leaves, torn up if they are big. Season with salt and lots of black pepper. Set aside until needed, when it must be reheated (should you have made more than you need, freeze the rest for another occasion).

Heat the rest of the oil in a large frying pan. Dust the fillets in seasoned flour and add them a few at a time, turning them once to colour both sides. Set them aside in a heatproof dish and keep warm until all are done.

When all the fish is cooked, reheat the sauce and pour it over the fish. Gently coat them with it, garnish with the black olives for colour contrast and serve with crusty Italian bread.

OPTIONS

*Brill (pictured), chicken turbot, halibut, John Dory, plaice, sea bass, sole*

6 large or 12 small skinned fish fillets, about 1kg/2¼lb in total, each folded across in half

175ml/6fl oz olive oil

½ garlic clove, chopped or sliced

675g/1½lb tomatoes, skinned and deseeded

4 tablespoons white wine

8-10 large fresh basil leaves

seasoned flour, for dusting

salt and freshly ground black pepper

6 black olives, to garnish

# Pan-fried Fish Fillets with Mushrooms, Garlic and Parsley

OPTIONS
*Brill, chicken turbot,
halibut, John Dory, plaice,
sea bass, sole*

6 skinned fish fillets,
each weighing about 115g/4oz
(or the equivalent to
1 kg/2¼lb of fish)

4 tablespoons grapeseed or
groundnut oil

4 tablespoons melted butter

1 garlic clove, crushed

150ml/¼ pint white wine

150ml/¼ pint fish stock (page 183)

175g/6oz button (or wild)
mushrooms, thinly sliced

450g/1lb chopped parsley

salt and freshly ground black pepper

*Mushrooms always soak up loads of butter or oil at the beginning of cooking before releasing it together with their own juices as they soften while they cook. A squeeze of lemon juice helps to keep the mushroom juices from blackening everything – but use only a very little or the mixture will be too sour.*

In a frying pan, gently heat the oil and butter. Add the garlic and let it sweat to soften it.

Add the wine and boil it down until it nearly all disappears. Add the stock and simmer to an emulsion.

Cook the mushrooms in this butter and oil mixture with a little salt and a squeeze of lemon diluted with 1 tablespoon of water. Simmer them until they release their juices into the liquid.

Throw in the chopped parsley and poach the fish in this mixture, basting them with the juices until they are set. This should only take a matter of minutes. Should the fish release a great deal of liquid, pour the liquid off and rapidly boil it down in a separate pan until an emulsion is achieved. Adjust the seasoning if necessary. Pour this back over the fish to serve.

Serve the fish with the mushrooms piled on top.

# Fish Fillets with Broad Beans in a Cream Sauce

*Middle-aged shelled broad beans can be rejuvenated by removing the tough grey outer skins. The beans make a delicious accompaniment to fish in a cream sauce.*

Cook the beans in rapidly boiling salted water until the centre is just tender, then refresh them in cold water. Slip off and discard their outer shells.

Simmer together the butter, shallots and wine until syrupy. Add the fish stock and bring the mixture to the boil, then strain over the fish in a saucepan.

Poach the fish in this until firm, 5-6 minutes. Lift it out, draining well, and keep warm.

Reduce the liquid in the pan to about 100 ml/3½ fl oz. Add the cream and simmer until it is thick enough to coat the back of a spoon. Season well with plenty of salt and pepper.

Fold the fish, beans and chopped chervil into the sauce and serve hot.

*Variation*: cut the fish into bite-sized pieces. Add the yolks of 2 eggs to the sauce with the fish and beans. Pile it all into cocotte dishes and simmer in a very slow oven (110°C/230°F/gas¼) until set, about half an hour. Turn out and serve hot, or chill and serve with salad for lunch.

OPTIONS
*Bream, brill, chicken turbot, John Dory, plaice, soles*

6 fish fillets,
each weighing about 115g/4oz

350g/12oz fresh broad beans

30g/1oz butter

2 shallots, chopped

150ml/¼ pint white wine

300ml/½ pint fish stock (page 183)

150ml/¼ pint double cream

1 tablespoon chopped chervil

salt and freshly ground black pepper

# Fish Fillets in a Spiced Cream Sauce

*This recipe demonstrates the technique of browning a cream reduction sauce by adding a beaten egg yolk to produce a professional glaze. If you put a cream sauce without egg under a grill, it will boil away to a fatty mess.*

In a large frying pan, simmer the shallots in all but 15g/½oz of the butter with a couple of tablespoons of water until the water has evaporated. Add the spices and cook for a further 2-3 minutes.

Pour in the vermouth and boil to reduce by two-thirds. Add the fish stock and crème fraîche. Season, reduce the heat to a simmer and poach the fillets in the mixture, in two batches if necessary, until just firm. Drain the fish and keep warm.

Make a beurre manié by kneading together the remaining butter with the flour, add this to the pan and bring to the boil, stirring continuously. Remove from the heat. Preheat the grill.

In a bowl with a whisk, beat the egg yolks with 2 teaspoons of water until frothy. (Do this preferably over a gentle heat, say set over a pan of barely simmering water, but not touching the water, and do not cook it so much that it scrambles; if in doubt, leave this bit of cooking out!) Fold the froth into the sauce and adjust the seasoning if necessary.

The fish may now be plated and browned individually if your grill is large enough. Otherwise, lay the fillets out on an ovenproof dish, slightly overlapping if necessary, and cover with the sauce to brown.

Serve with broccoli and new potatoes.

OPTIONS
*Bream, brill (pictured)*

6 large or 12 small skinned fish fillets

2 shallots, finely chopped

75g/2½ oz butter

1 tablespoon paprika

1 teaspoon ground cumin

1 teaspoon ground coriander seeds

150ml/¼ pint Noilly Prat white vermouth

300ml/½ pint fish stock (page 183)

15g/½oz flour

1 tub (200ml/7fl oz) crème fraîche or 150ml/¼ pint whipping cream

2 egg yolks

salt and freshly ground black pepper

# Small Fillets of Fish in White Wine Sauce

OPTIONS
*Dab, John Dory,
plaice, red mullet,
trout, whiting*

12 fish fillets, about 1.25kg/2½lb
in total

85g/3oz butter, plus more for
greasing

150ml/¼ pint Noilly Prat white
vermouth

2 shallots, finely chopped

450ml/¾ pint fish stock (page 183)

30g/1oz flour

2 egg yolks

4 tablespoons whipping cream

salt and freshly ground black pepper

few peeled cooked prawns, to
garnish (optional)

handful of grapes, to garnish
(optional)

*Small round fish like trout often come filleted and sometimes it is more convenient to cook plaice, dab or other flat fish off the bone. It's quicker and also less messy for the cook!*

Preheat the oven to 190°C/375°F/gas5.

Remove all skin from the fillets (unless they are filleted red mullets, which you must scale). Lay the fillets in a buttered, shallow ovenproof dish.

In a small pan, reduce the vermouth with the shallots and 50g/2oz of the butter and, when it is syrupy, add the stock and simmer for 5 minutes.

Strain this over the fish, pressing out as much flavour as possible from the shallots. Cover with foil and bake for 5-8 minutes, until the fish has just set.

Meanwhile, rinse the pan and melt the remaining butter in it. Add the flour and cook, stirring for 30 seconds. Now pour the juices from the fish back into the pan and whisk into the roux. Simmer to reduce to about 300 ml/½ pint. Preheat the grill.

Whisk up the egg yolks with the cream and add to the reduction. Bring nearly to the boil, whisking all the time, adjust the seasoning if necessary and pour over the fillets, perhaps adding a few peeled cooked prawns and some grapes. Brown under the grill and serve with steamed broccoli florets.

# Rolled Fish Fillets in Tarragon Sauce

*This light dish with lots of taste can use any fillets, since they are rolled and won't break up if you lift them carefully. The amount of liquid they exude varies with the fish used, but you can always boil away too much and thus concentrate the flavour.*

In a little oil, fry together the shallots, 1 of the garlic cloves and the tomatoes. Add the vinegar and reduce right down. Add the sugar, mustard and tarragon and season.

Roll the fillets into paupiettes (see page 21), tucking the mixture around them. Place them in a baking tin which will hold them snugly in a single layer and dot with butter.

Pour in the stock, cover and cook gently in the oven until they set, 6-8 minutes.

Remove from the oven, pour off the juices and boil them down to a sauce-like consistency.

Meanwhile fry the breadcrumbs with the remaining garlic in a little more oil, stirring well, until crisp.

Plate the fish, pour the sauce around it and sprinkle with some of the fried breadcrumbs.

OPTIONS
*Fillets of any fish*

6 skinned fish fillets, each weighing about 115g/4oz

2 shallots, finely chopped

2 garlic cloves, crushed

2 tomatoes, skinned, deseeded and chopped

1 tablespoon tarragon vinegar

1 tablespoon sugar

1 teaspoon Dijon mustard

1 tablespoon chopped fresh tarragon

175g/6oz butter

150ml/¼ pint fish stock (page 183)

50g/2oz fresh breadcrumbs

salt and freshly ground black pepper

grapeseed or groundnut oil, for frying

# Fish with Mixed Vegetables in Sour Cream Sauce

OPTIONS
*Small cod, John Dory,
plaice, soles, trout*

12 skinned fish fillets,
each weighing about 85g/3oz,
folded in half

12 baby carrots

2 yellow courgettes

5 tablespoons grapeseed or
groundnut oil

50g/2oz butter

1 onion, chopped

½ red sweet pepper,
deseeded and chopped

150ml/¼ pint white wine

150ml/¼ pint fish stock (page 183)

1 tub (200ml/7fl oz) sour cream
or crème fraîche

125g/4½oz spinach

*This colourful dish incorporates a variety of vegetables in a tangy sauce to bind them. Some types of crème fraîche don't thicken very well when boiled, so an egg yolk stirred in at the end will help give the sauce the right coating consistency.*

Cook the carrots in boiling salted water until just tender and refresh them in cold water.

Slice the courgettes and sear them in a large pan in a mixture of the oil and butter. Remove with a slotted spoon and set aside.

Now just stiffen the pieces of seasoned fish in the oil and butter and lift them out. Set aside.

Add the chopped onion and red pepper and cook gently until they soften. Add the wine and reduce the liquid to about 1 tablespoon. Pour in the fish stock and reduce by half.

Add the cream and bring to the boil. Season, add the spinach and carrots and return the courgettes and fish to the pan. Simmer everything together gently for 2 minutes, adding water if the sauce becomes too thick. Alternatively, if the sauce has not thickened, stir in a lightly beaten egg yolk.

Serve the fish with the vegetables around them.

# Fish Fillets with Red Cabbage and Apple

*This dish will work either with a whole unfilleted flat fish, such as John Dory or chicken turbot, or with fillets rolled into paupiettes as below.*

Preheat the oven to 190°C/375°F/gas5. Season the fish and if using fillets roll them into paupiettes.

Cut the bacon into little pieces and dry-fry them over a moderate to high heat in a large pan to release the fat. Add the oil and the sliced onion and cook for 2 minutes.

While the onion is cooking, remove any tough stalks and core from the cabbage and slice the leaves into thin strips. Add these to the pan, together with the vinegar, 2 tablespoons of water, the cloves and bay leaves. Boil fiercely for about 20 seconds and then turn down the heat and simmer gently until the cabbage is cooked, say about 20 minutes.

Remove the cloves and the bay leaves. Peel and core the apple. Dice the flesh and add it to the pan.

Place the mixture in a single layer on the bottom of a large ovenproof dish, then lay the fish on top. Cover with foil and bake for 5 to 10 minutes, until the fish has cooked through (it will feel firm when lightly pressed).

OPTIONS

*Chicken turbot, John Dory or any fillets*

6 large or 12 small skinned fish fillets, or 6 small whole fish

4 slices of streaky bacon

1 tablespoon grapeseed or groundnut oil

1 onion, thinly sliced

¼ red cabbage

1 tablespoon white wine vinegar

2 cloves

2 bay leaves

1 firm eating apple

salt and freshly ground black pepper

# Fish Fillets with Duxelles en Cocotte

OPTIONS

*Lemon sole (pictured), small brill, cod, dab, haddock, plaice, bream, sole, whiting*

12 small skinned fillets or 6 large ones

140g/5oz butter

salt and freshly ground black pepper

parsley, to garnish

*for the duxelles:*
225g/8oz finely chopped onions

115g/4oz butter

225g/8oz finely chopped mushrooms

2 uncoated or well-scrubbed lemons

freshly grated nutmeg to taste

2-3 fresh thyme leaves (lemon thyme if possible)

*This simple delicious preparation works with any fillet. The better the flavour of the fish, the better the dish. It provides an excellent way of learning to appreciate the differences in flavour of different types of fish, but make sure the fillets are very fresh or this preparation will show up any staleness.*

Preheat the oven to 200°C/400°F/gas6 and butter 6 ramekins.

Make the duxelles: grate the zest from the lemons. In a large frying pan simmer the onions in 150ml/¼ pint water with the butter until the water evaporates and the onions begin to fry, but do not allow the onions to brown.

Add the mushrooms, cook for 1 minute, then add the lemon zest, nutmeg, thyme and some seasoning. Cook this mixture until it dries out and starts to fry again.

Season the fish fillets and curl them loosely inside the buttered ramekins, then tuck the duxelles in and around them. Dot each with a knob of butter. Slice each lemon across into 3 rounds and lay one on top of each ramekin. Bake in the oven for 15 minutes.

To serve, squeeze the hot lemon slice over the fish and discard it. Decorate with a sprig of parsley and serve.

# Fish Fillets with Crab Filling and Beurre Noisette

*This crab mixture can be cooked and served as a savoury custard. Turn it out and serve it, either hot or cold, with a light hollandaise sauce (page 184). As this is a splendid recipe to prepare in advance, it is perfect for dinner parties and looks particularly marvellous when made with pink rainbow trout. Anchovy essence is a useful seasoning, but you could easily substitute* nam pla, *the Thai fish sauce which performs the same duty in the cooking of South-east Asia – as a seasoning rather than a flavouring.*

Preheat the oven to 120°C/250°F/gas½ and line a small deep baking tin with cling film.

Make a roux by melting 50g/2oz of the butter in saucepan, stirring in the flour and cooking for a few minutes, stirring. Stir in the milk and cook to make a smooth sauce.

In a liquidizer or food processor, blend this with the crab and eggs and season to taste with the anchovy essence.

Pour into the prepared tin and cook gently for about 1 hour, until set. Allow to cool and turn out when needed.

Lay each fillet flat, skinned side up, and season well. Cut a square of stuffing to fit in the middle of each fillet. Fold over the ends, turn the whole thing over and allow it to rest in a cool place.

Meanwhile, make a noisette butter with half the remaining butter by gently heating it in a small pan until it is a nutty brown. Then add the vinegar and allow the strong vapour to boil away, leaving just the flavoured butter.

Heat the rest of the butter in a frying pan, dust the fish 'parcels' in seasoned flour and cook them quickly on each side, starting with the 'join' down and then cooking the upper side long enough to produce an attractive brown colour (about 3 minutes a side).

Transfer the fillets to warmed plates, sprinkle with chopped tarragon or parsley and spoon the reheated noisette butter over. Serve on a bed of steamed or grilled asparagus tips if you wish.

OPTIONS

*Bream, brill, chicken turbot, grey mullet, halibut, mackerel, plaice, rainbow trout (pictured), sea bass, soles*

6 skinned fish fillets, each weighing 115-140g/4-5oz

285g/10oz butter (slightly salted)

100g/3½oz flour

600ml/1 pint milk

225g/8oz dark crab meat

4 eggs, plus 4 extra yolks

2-3 teaspoons anchovy essence

few drops of white wine vinegar

seasoned flour, for dusting

salt and freshly ground black pepper

chopped tarragon or parsley, to garnish

steamed or grilled asparagus tips, to serve (optional)

# Fish with Cucumber Olives, Butter and Herbs

OPTIONS
*Brill, chicken turbot,*
*John Dory, plaice, sole*

3 flat fish, each weighing about
675g/1½lb, trimmed

2 cucumbers

115g/4oz slightly salted butter

850ml/1½ pints fish stock (page 183)

1 tablespoon chopped dill,
parsley and chives

plenty of pepper

*Every now and then there is a glut of cucumber and they become very cheap, so it is worth using them as a vegetable instead of just in salads. They stay firmer than marrow when cooked, and have a delicate flavour that goes well with fish.*

Peel the cucumbers and halve them lengthwise, then cut each half lengthwise into three long strips. Cut away the seeds and slice the strips into 2.5cm/1in chunks. Trim these into 'olives' (oval-shaped like olive stones) if you like, or leave them as they are. Stew them in half the butter until they are just softened.

Poach the fish whole in the stock until stiff, about 5-7 minutes. Drain, remove the skin and lift off the fillets. Put these in an oval baking dish, cover with foil and keep warm.

Strain the juices into a pan and reduce to 300ml/½ pint. Add the remaining butter and cucumber pieces with their liquid. Season with plenty of pepper and some salt if necessary.

When you are ready to serve, bring the cucumber mixture to the boil, throw in the chopped herbs and pour the mixture over the fish fillets.

Serve straight from the dish or arrange on individual plates, scattering the cucumber around the fish.

# Fish Fillets Wrapped in Courgette Ribbons

*This is a particularly attractive way of presenting this dish and the flavour of the butter can be changed to say lemon and tarragon, or chive and parsley, or even curry... the choice is yours.*

First make the anchovy butter: in a blender, purée the drained anchovies with the softened butter. Set aside.

Reduce the vermouth in 140g/5oz of the butter by about three-quarters. Add the stock and boil down to about 300ml/½ pint.

Preheat the oven to 180°C/350°F/gas4 if baking this dish. With a potato peeler, cut the courgettes into ribbons. Cook these in the remaining butter until pliable. Season.

Season the fish portions, spread anchovy butter on them and wrap them up in the courgette ribbons, overlapping the edges like bandages.

Arrange, with the join underneath, in an ovenproof dish. Pour in the reduced stock mixture and bake for 10 minutes (or pan-fry in the stock mixture, covered with a lid, for 5 minutes). Baste for the last 5 minutes and add a little water if the juices become too buttery.

OPTIONS
*Cod, halibut, salmon
or fillets of other plump round fish*

1 large boned and skinned side of fish, weighing about 900g/2lb, cut into 6 portions

150ml/¼ pint Noilly Prat white vermouth

175g/6oz butter

300ml/½ pint fish stock (page 183)

3 courgettes, each about 17.5cm/7in

salt and freshly ground black pepper

parsley, to garnish

*for the anchovy butter:*
1 small tin (50g/2oz) of anchovies in oil

140g/5oz softened butter

# Gratin of Fish Fillets, Spinach and Aubergine in Béchamel Sauce

OPTIONS
*Small brill, John Dory,
plaice, sole, whiting*

12 skinned fish fillets,
each weighing about 85g/3oz

1 large onion

125ml/4fl oz grapeseed or
groundnut oil

675g/1½lb aubergines, sliced

1 tablespoon chopped marjoram

125g/4½oz spinach

50g/2oz flour

150ml/¼ pint milk

150ml/¼ pint whipping cream

freshly grated nutmeg to taste

50g/2oz grated Cheddar cheese

salt and freshly ground black pepper

*This may seem an old-fashioned recipe, but it is a classic way of presenting fish and also very comforting. Simmering the sauce until it is the right consistency matures the flour, which makes such a difference to the final flavour of the dish.*

In 300ml/½ pint of water, simmer the whole unpeeled onion for 20 minutes until it is soft. Drain, retaining the water. Peel and slice the onion and put aside.

Preheat the oven to 230°C/450°F/gas8 and season the fish fillets well with salt and pepper.

Brush a large heavy non-stick pan well with oil and heat it. Keeping the heat high, place the aubergine slices in the pan in a single layer. Turn the slices after 2 minutes to let them soften on the other side as well. Season.

Now lay the aubergine slices in an ovenproof dish, overlapping slightly, and sprinkle them with the marjoram. Lay the fish on top.

Fry the spinach in 1 tablespoon of oil in the pan, then tuck it in around the fish in little piles.

Heat about 5 tablespoons of oil in the pan, stir in the flour and cook briefly, stirring. Pour in the onion water, milk and cream. Whisk together and simmer until the mixture coats the back of a spoon. Add the sliced onion, some freshly grated nutmeg and seasoning.

Pour the sauce over the fish, sprinkle with the cheese and brown in the oven for about 15 minutes, finishing off the browning under a preheated hot grill if necessary.

# Gratin of Marinated Fish Topped with a Courgette Crust

*With its fascinating flavour – the essence of a red wine vinegar has a rather pungent kick, but the courgette crust on top helps to soften and contrast with the acidity – this is an excellent recipe for some of the humbler fishes.*

In a large pan, melt the butter with the vinegar and reduce the vinegar in butter until it forms a thick glaze.

Add the fish stock and simmer together until the stock is reduced by half. Season.

Poach the fillets gently in this enriched stock for 5 minutes and leave to cool in the stock for half an hour.

Lift the fillets out of the stock, season and place them in a buttered oven dish. If necessary, reduce the stock to 150ml/¼ pint and pour it over the fillets.

Meanwhile, grate or finely chop the courgettes and fry them in 2 tablespoons of the oil with the garlic and herbs. At the same time, in another pan, brown the breadcrumbs in the remaining oil. When the courgettes have softened and lost most of their water, season and pile them on top of the fish. Sprinkle the browned breadcrumbs over the lot.

OPTIONS
*Dab, plaice, pollack, whiting*

6 large or 12 small skinned fillets

115g/4oz butter,
plus more for the dish

250ml/8fl oz red wine vinegar

450ml/¾ pint fish stock (page 183)

4 medium courgettes

100ml/3½fl oz olive oil

2 garlic cloves, sliced

3-4 basil leaves

½ teaspoon dried sage

50g/2oz breadcrumbs

# Deep-fried Fish in Batter with Tartare Sauce

*The recipe for batter given here produces a crunchy light coating as there are no egg yolks in it, only the whites. It is important to get the oil to the right temperature as the batter will then quickly make an oil-proof seal around the fish to prevent it getting greasy, while keeping it naturally moist and juicy. For this reason, don't put too many pieces of fish into the oil at one time or the temperature will drop and the batter seal will not form quickly enough. Serve the fish with this heavenly garlicky tartare as a dip.*

First make the sauce: in a blender or food processor, whisk together the egg yolks, mustard, salt, water and crushed garlic for 3 minutes or so until the mixture becomes pale.

Pour in the first spoonful of oil and allow it to be absorbed (5 seconds), then the next (another 5 seconds), then more and more but pausing each time in between to let the mixture 'digest' each spoonful. The sauce should be very thick.

Chop up the gherkins and capers, dry them by patting them with paper towel and fold them in.

Now make the batter: mix together the flour, salt and oil and add half the water. Blend until smooth and thin out with the rest of the water. Just before use, beat the egg whites until they hold their shape and fold them in.

To fry the fish, the oil must be very hot but not smoking (about 180°C/350°F). Test it with a cube of bread, which should begin to brown in 3 seconds. Use a deep-fryer for safety, if possible, also a draining basket for lifting the fish out. Remove the fish from the oil when golden grown and allow excess oil to drain back into the pan. Drain the pieces briefly on paper towel and season with salt. Cool and strain your oil before storing it for further use.

Serve the fish with chips and the tartare sauce in a bowl.

OPTIONS
*Any fish fillets*

1.25kg/2½lb skinned fish fillets

grapeseed or groundnut oil, for deep-frying

salt

*for the batter:*
4 tablespoons flour

1 teaspoon salt

1 tablespoon grapeseed or groundnut oil

150ml/¼ pint water

whites of 2 eggs

*for the garlic tartare sauce:*
3 egg yolks

1 teaspoon Dijon mustard

salt to taste

1 teaspoon water

2 garlic cloves, crushed

350ml/12fl oz grapeseed or groundnut oil

3 gherkins

1 tablespoon capers

# Baked Fish Layered with Bacon and Mixed Vegetables

OPTIONS
*Brill, chicken turbot, halibut,
John Dory, plaice, sea bass, sole*

1 whole fish, weighing about
1.25kg/2½lb, filleted and skinned,
or 675g/1½lb fish fillets

1 carrot, finely chopped

1 onion, chopped

1 celery stalk, finely chopped

4 tablespoons olive oil

115g/4oz chopped mushrooms

about 300ml/½ pint white wine

½ teaspoon dried thyme

2 tomatoes, skinned,
deseeded and chopped

2 thick rashers of
sweet-cure bacon, finely diced

150ml/¼ pint fish stock (page 183)

50/2oz butter

salt and freshly ground black pepper

1 tablespoon chopped parsley,
to garnish

*Serve this really flavoursome satisfying dish with new potatoes
and broccoli for a family supper. Add a few cooked peeled prawns
to the sauce at the last minute for a special occasion.*

Preheat the oven to 190°C/375°F/gas5.

Cook together the carrot, onion and celery in the oil. When they have softened, add the mushrooms and cook until dry. Add the wine and reduce to a syrupy consistency. Mix in the thyme, tomato flesh and bacon. Reheat and season.

Season the fish. Then in an ovenproof dish place a layer of half the fillets. Lay two-thirds of the vegetable mix on top. Follow this with another layer of the rest of the fish and scatter over that the rest of the vegetable mix. Pour the fish stock around the fish and finally dot the top with knobs of the butter. Cover and cook in the oven for 25 minutes.

Remove from the oven, pour off the liquid into a small pan and reduce to a sauce. Pour this over the fish. Slice the fish across into six portions and sprinkle with the parsley to serve.

# Caribbean Baked Fish

*This recipe is included at the request of Mrs Leventhorpe in the Isle of Man. I personally enjoy the tang of mango with fish but I do appreciate that it is not to everyone's taste. The bananas add a sweetness.*

Cut the mango in half flat against the flat central stone, then keeping the knife flat and the sharp edge away from you, remove the flesh from the skin. Cut the flesh into cubes. Peel the bananas and slice each lengthwise into 3 long strips.

In a small pan, boil together the coconut milk, ginger, raisins and lemon zest until the mixture becomes well scented and slightly reduced.

In a large frying pan, fry the banana strips in a little hot oil for about 15 seconds on each side and then brush them with the lemon juice. Lay them flat on a work surface and place a seasoned fish fillet on each one. Tie together with a ribbon of ham.

Place the banana and fish parcels back in the frying pan, sprinkle the mango cubes over them and strain the coconut milk over the top. Cook gently, basting, for 5 minutes.

Serve on warmed individual plates with a little of the sauce poured over each portion.

OPTIONS

*Brill, chicken turbot, halibut, John Dory, sole*

12 skinned fish fillets, each weighing about 50-85g/2-3oz

1 mango

4 under-ripe bananas

1 tin (400ml/14fl oz) of coconut milk

30g/1oz root ginger, scraped and sliced

few raisins

grated zest of 1 lemon, plus 1 teaspoon juice

225g/8oz thinly sliced ham

salt and freshly ground black pepper

grapeseed or groundnut oil, for frying

# Fish Fillets Topped with Spring Greens and Rolled in Pancakes

OPTIONS
*Small bass, dab,
cheaper sole, whiting*

6 skinless fish fillets,
each weighing about 115g/4oz

50g/2oz butter

675g/1½lb cooked spring greens

freshly grated nutmeg to taste

chopped parsley, to garnish

salt and freshly ground black pepper

grapeseed or groundnut oil,
for frying

*for the pancake batter:*
350ml/12fl oz milk

2 eggs

115g/4oz flour

50g/2oz melted butter

*for the lemon sauce:*
1 lemon

140g/5oz melted butter

100ml/3½fl oz fish stock (page 183)

*Pancakes are an irritation to make – but if you set aside an hour to make 3-4 dozen, you can freeze them, layered with film, and keep them in batches of 6 or 12 (according to the size of your appetite and your dinner parties!)*

*Spring greens seem extraordinary with fish, but they are absolutely delicious with butter and nutmeg, instead of the usual spinach.*

First make the pancake batter: whizz together in the blender or food processor the milk and eggs, then mix in the flour and melted butter. Season with salt and pepper.

Lightly brush an 18cm/7in crêpe pan with oil and heat until fairly hot. Pour in just enough batter to coat the base of the pan, tilting the pan to spread it evenly. Cook briskly until bubbles start to appear on top of the pancake. Then turn the pancake over and cook the other side until just golden brown. Keep the cooked pancake warm while cooking the remaining 5 pancakes in the same way, wiping out the pan with a wad of paper towels and brushing it afresh with oil each time.

Make the lemon sauce: zest the lemon and mix with its juice and all the other ingredients in a small pan. Season to taste and bring to the boil.

Now assemble the dish: melt the butter in a frying pan. Chop up the spring greens finely. Add them to the butter with a good grinding of nutmeg. Season and mix well.

Lay each fillet at one end of a pancake, pile some spring greens on top and roll each one up firmly. Place the rolled pancakes in an ovenproof dish and pour the lemon sauce over them. Top up with a little water if necessary to half cover the pancakes. Cook in a hot oven for about 8-10 minutes.

When the pancakes are crisp on top, lift them out, put them on individual plates. Pour the sauce, reduced if necessary, over them and garnish some chopped parsley before serving.

# Stuffed Fillets in Filo

*Buy only the best Greek filo pastry. As there is no fat in filo, always brush the sheets of pastry with lots of butter to give a rich crunchy effect. As it dries so quickly and can then tear readily, work with one sheet at a time, keeping the others rolled up in their wrappings or under a damp tea towel.*

Preheat the oven to 200°C/400°F/gas6 and season the fish fillets.

Make the stuffing: in a large frying pan, cook the onions in half the butter with 2 tablespoons of water until soft. Add the mushrooms, thyme, bay leaf, lemon juice and zest. Season to taste with salt, pepper and freshly grated nutmeg. Cook everything together for 5 minutes until the mixture has dried out and is becoming buttery. Allow to cool a little and add one of the eggs, lightly beaten.

Melt the remaining butter. Lay out flat one sheet of the filo and brush it generously with the melted butter. Then quickly place a fillet at one edge, top it with one-sixth of the stuffing and roll up neatly into the shape of a cracker. Trim the ends and brush the top with some of the remaining egg, beaten. Repeat with the other sheets of pastry and fillets.

As soon as possible, bake in the oven until crisp and golden, about 15 minutes.

OPTIONS
*Bream, brill, chicken turbot, halibut, hokey, John Dory, plaice, sea bass, sole*

6 fish fillets,
each weighing about 115g/4oz,
skinned or scaled

2 medium onions, chopped

175g/6oz butter

50g/2oz button mushrooms, sliced

½ teaspoon fresh thyme

bay leaf

zest and 1 teaspoon juice
from 1 lemon

freshly grated nutmeg

2 eggs

6 sheets of filo pastry

salt and freshly ground black pepper

# Tartlets of Mushroom and Flat Fish

*These tasty tartlets make a perfect first course for a dinner party. They are also very practical in that they may be prepared in advance, but assembled at the last minute.*

Preheat the oven to 190°C/375°F/gas5. Shell the tiger prawns, reserving the shells, and cut them across in half. Season well with salt and pepper and set aside.

Fry half the onions in half the butter until the onion begins to take on a little colour. Now add the chopped mushrooms and cook them briskly to boil off their water. Mix in the prawns, season again and set aside.

Melt the rest of the butter in a saucepan, add the reserved shells with the remaining onion and cook until the onions are soft. Add the white wine and reduce to a syrup. Add 450ml/¾pint water and simmer together for 5 minutes.

Put the fish in an ovenproof dish and pour this liquid over the fish. Cook in the oven until the fillets may be lifted off, about 15 minutes.

Preheat the grill. Strain the liquid from the fish into a pan and reduce to about 200ml/7fl oz. Beat a little of this into the egg yolk mixed with the flour and return it to the pan. Add the mustard, parsley and chives, season and bring nearly to the boil again.

Removing the skin first, lift the fish fillets from the bone. Slice the fillets diagonally into diamond shapes and warm them up in the sauce. Thin out with a little milk if necessary.

Divide the mushroom mixture between the tartlet cases, spoon the fish mixture on top and brown under the grill. Serve warm, garnished with purple basil and radicchio leaves if you wish.

OPTIONS
*Any flat fish*

9 small tiger prawns

675g/1½lb whole flat fish

2 onions, chopped

85g/3oz butter

115g/4oz mushrooms, chopped

150ml/¼ pint white wine

1 egg yolk

½ teaspoon flour

1 teaspoon French mustard

1 tablespoon chopped parsley

½ tablespoon chopped chives

6 small (8.5cm/3½in) shortcrust tartlet cases, baked blind (see overleaf)

salt and freshly ground black pepper

purple basil and radicchio leaves, to garnish (optional)

# Family Picnic Flan

OPTIONS
*Any fish*

6 medium skinned fillets
of smoked or plain fish

350g/12oz shortcrust pastry

4 eggs, plus 1 extra yolk
for the pastry

zest and juice of 1 lemon

450g/1lb cooked spring greens

freshly grated nutmeg to taste

85g/3oz butter

150ml/¼ pint yoghurt or whipping
cream

115g/4oz grated Cheddar cheese

salt and freshly ground black pepper

*This one dish contains all the protein, carbohydrates and vitamins you need in one day; well perhaps not quite all, but it does make any plain or smoked fish into a balanced meal-in-one.*

First prepare the pastry case which must be 'baked blind'. Preheat the oven to 200°C/400°F/gas6. Roll the pastry out until thin and use it to line a 25cm/10in flan tin. Prick the base of the shell with a fork. If you have another similar tin, lay it inside and weight it down, or line the pastry case with greaseproof paper or foil and fill it with dried beans or similar.

Bake until set and lightly coloured around the edges, about 15-20 minutes. Remove the weights and any lining paper or foil and brush the insides of the pastry case with egg yolk to seal it. Return to the oven for about 5 minutes more to dry the pastry off.

While the pastry case is baking, sprinkle the fish with the lemon zest and season. Curl the fillets into rolls, wrap securely in cling film and steam for 5 minutes. Put aside to allow to set and cool a little. Slice them in half if they are very large.

Squeeze the greens well to get rid of any excess moisture and heat them together with the nutmeg and butter in a pan over a gentle heat, stirring, until the residual moisture has evaporated. Season well. Put aside to allow to cool a little.

In a bowl, beat the eggs, add the yoghurt or cream with lemon juice to taste and mix with the greens.

Pour the mixture into the prepared pastry case. Remove the film from the fish fillets and tuck them into the greens. Sprinkle with the cheese and bake for 15 to 20 minutes until the mixture has set.

If necessary, grill the cheese for another minute or so to finish the melting and browning.

# Open Fish Pasty

*Pasties are not known for their lightness. However, give them more filling than pastry, open them up and you have a sort of potato tart. It can look very appetizing made in layers. Allowing it to cool before cutting gives the starch time to set and keep the juices in. You can reheat it to serve or just eat it cold.*

*To bake my pastry case blind, instead of resorting to dried beans (see opposite), I have a small non-stick ovenproof saucepan which I line with pastry, then with foil and fit another pan inside to keep the sides up. When it goes under the grill to brown the filling at the end, it is easy to handle with an oven glove. If you try this, don't forget that the handle of the pan has to be ovenproof too!*

Blanch the spinach briefly in boiling salted water, especially if it is the tough kind. Drain and set aside.

Melt half the butter in a large frying pan and soften the potatoes in it, slipping the slices into the pan one after the other to prevent them sticking together and adding 150ml/¼ pint water and some salt. The water will boil away as the potatoes cook, leaving soft buttery slices. Arrange half of these on the pastry base, setting the rest aside.

Add the rest of the butter to the pan. Add the onions and some seasoning and cook them a little until just soft. Lay half of these on top of the potatoes. Add the thyme, lemon juice and nutmeg to those in the pan. Cook for a moment to mix these flavourings in well.

Next place a layer of half the spinach in the tart over the onions. Then arrange the fillets evenly around the pastry. Season and top with the lemony onions, then with the rest of the spinach.

Return the reserved potatoes to the frying pan and add the milk. Boil most of this off and arrange the potato slices tastefully, overlapping around the top (like apple slices in an apple tart).

Cook the tart in the oven for about 30 minutes, pressing the filling down once halfway through to compact it. If necessary, brown the filling under the grill to finish. Allow to cool before slicing cold or reheated.

OPTIONS
*Fillets of any fish*

350g/12oz skinned fish fillets

50g/2oz spinach

115g/4oz butter

450g/1lb potatoes, thinly sliced

1 medium (25cm/10in) shortcrust pastry case, baked blind (see opposite)

225g/8oz onions, thinly sliced

½ teaspoon dried thyme

juice of ½ lemon

freshly grated nutmeg to taste

150ml/¼ pint milk

salt and freshly ground black pepper

# Jellied Fish Terrine

OPTIONS
*Bream, brill, chicken turbot,*
*John Dory, plaice, sole*

1.8kg/4lb flat fish on the bone

4 medium carrots, peeled,
cut into strips and cooked

1 red and 1 green sweet pepper

300ml/½ pint Noilly Prat
white vermouth

850ml/1½ pints fish stock
(page 183)

½ teaspoon salt

whites of 2 eggs

6 leaves of gelatine
or an 11g sachet (enough to set
600ml/1 pint)

*This is an attractive way of serving a fish course at a dinner party, especially in the summer as all the work is done in advance. Chill the plates as well and, with a salad dressed with a vinaigrette, this does indeed make a good light lunch on its own. Do, however, give yourself plenty of time to make it – it always takes longer than one expects.*

Preheat the oven to 190°C/375°F/gas5 and a hot grill. Cut the carrots and peppers into long batons. Blister the peppers uniformly under the grill, then transfer to a zip-lock bag and leave to steam for a few minutes. Peel off the charred skin and cut the flesh into strips.

Place the fish in a single layer in a large baking tin (if this is not possible, cook in two batches).

In a saucepan, boil the vermouth to reduce it by about three-quarters. Add the fish stock and pour the mixture over the fish. Top up with enough hot water to cover and add the salt. Cook the fish in the oven for 10 to 20 minutes, checking after 10 minutes to see when it will lift off the bone, returning it to the heat until it does. Pour off the resulting stock through a sieve.

Fillet the fish and discard all skin and bone, but keep any juices to add to the stock.

Clarify the stock by whisking the egg whites to a froth and folding them into the liquid. Heat the stock and allow it to bubble through the topping of egg froth. Turn the heat down and simmer for 5 minutes. Remove from the heat and allow the mixture to settle. Strain it through a cloth and repeat the procedure if the liquid is not clear.

Boil the strained stock to reduce it to about 575ml/1 pint and, when it has cooled a little, add the gelatine dissolved in a little water. Coat a 33cm/13in terrine, especially the base, with some of the jelly and allow this to set.

Dip the fillets one by one into the liquid jelly stock and arrange them in layers in the terrine. Each layer must be allowed to set before the next is put on top and a little hot jelly is poured in just before each new layer. This prevents the layers from splitting when they are cold. Intersperse the fish with strips of red and green pepper and carrots.

Place an oblong weight over the final layer (the base of another terrine, perhaps) just to submerge the fish and remove the bubbles. Chill overnight to set.

Dip the terrine very briefly in hot water to turn it out. Then slice with a knife dipped in hot water.

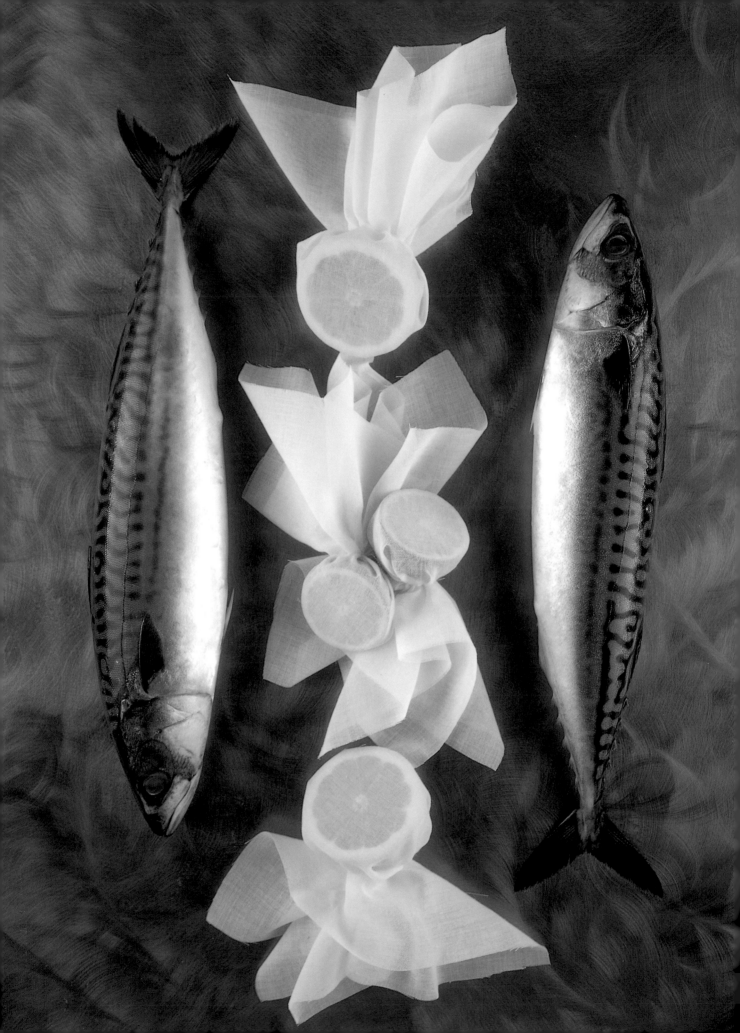

# round fish & cutlets

There is enormous diversity in this section both in size, with fish as small as whitebait and as large as meaty tuna, and in texture – from flaky white fish like cod to succulent oily fish like trout, salmon and mackerel

## TYPES OF ROUND FISH

Many round sea fish are sold small enough to cook as individual helpings – although the law prevents you buying certain fish, like bass, smaller than a statutory size to protect the species.

Freshwater farm-reared trout are the most popular freshwater fish and have the advantage of being caught only hours before being eaten. This is a distinct plus, but the flavour unfortunately doesn't have the same character as that of the wild ones. Farmed or wild, I think the most important aspect of this fish is that the skin is delicious and holds 50% of the flavour. Dusted with seasoned flour and fried quickly in butter, it is food for the Gods. This holds for almost every whole fish treated in this way.

The red mullet is a beauty, often with an intriguing elusive flavour uniquely its own. The smell reminds me of spices, and the deservedly celebrated liver has the biggest share of the flavour. There are other fish with delicious livers, like bass, but do not eat them indiscriminately or you may come a cropper – how about a good dose of cod liver?

It is interesting to divide fish into two categories – those with their oil in their flesh, like salmon, herring, etc., and those that keep it in their livers, e.g. cod, monkfish etc., as well as many flat fish. Cod's head, makes especially good non-oily stock.

## PREPARING ROUND FISH

Nearly all round fish – particularly the smaller specimens of sea fish – have scales that must be scraped off against the grain if you want to eat the skin, as they are unpleasant (if not impossible) to eat. Luckily it's what lies beneath the scales that really matters and here there is more choice in texture and flavour than with the flat family or, in my opinion, with all the other culinary sources of protein put together.

Many round fish normally grow to sizes that are too large for a family to eat in one go, but there's always the recipe that needs leftovers – from exotic terrines to fish cakes and flans. Then again the larger fish can be scaled or skinned and then filleted. A few years ago it was not possible to buy a section or

BASS – *Silvery grey fish with big scales and horrendous spikes or fins. Often mistaken for salmon, but totally different dry white flesh with delicious flavour. Few bones. Very expensive, partly due to low ratio of flesh to bone. Being farmed successfully. Best roasted whole. Scales.*

COD – *Generally large fish, but small also available. Greeny-brown mottled skin. Firm flesh which forms into large flakes. Distinctive pleasant fishy flavour.*

*Good for stock. Oily liver. Sold whole, filleted or in cutlets. Can be expensive. Few scales (edible).*

COLEY – *Darker-skinned relative of cod. Good flavour, but often unpopular because of dark flesh (which whitens on cooking), so cheap. Few scales (edible).*

GURNARD – *If it weren't for the many bones this would be popular for flavour. Grey- or red-coloured rough skin, heavy bony head. Scales. Cheap.*

HADDOCK – *Usually filleted. Fresh flavour and juicy flesh, which flakes easily. Popular fish, medium-priced. Few scales (edible).*

HAKE – *Distinctive soft flesh with few bones. Triangular backbone easily removed. Good cutlets when large. Spanish national fish. Medium-priced. Few scales (edible).*

HERRING – *Good flavour but oily, so usually grilled. Cheap. Easily boned and scaled.*

JOHN DORY – *Ugly appearance. It has a triple row of fins and bones along the outline of its flat body. Once these and the head are cut off the rest of the fish is easily dealt with. Beautiful firm flesh with excellent flavour, which falls into three small fillets or goujons each side. Few bones, no scales noticeable.*

MACKEREL – *Striped, non-scaly skin. Oily fish with good flavour and moist flesh, especially when very fresh. Easy to bone.*

even a side of salmon, but it is possible now. I don't think, though, that a fishmonger will sell a single side of bass, but undoubtedly he will fillet a whole fish for you, which you can share with someone else. In this way, dishes such as Fish Fillets Wrapped in Courgette Ribbons on page 41, which require a thick piece of a larger fish without skin or bones, can become practical. (This recipe is in the Flat Fish and Fillets chapter, as that contains my suggestions for using all kinds of fillets, flat and round.)

## COOKING CUTLETS

The other method of preparing round fish is to cut them right across, leaving a centre bone that will slip out easily when the fish is ready. These cutlets take longer to cook than fillets, and the skin cannot be removed beforehand, which is a plus as far as flavour and texture are concerned but a disadvantage for the 'bone-conscious-can't-think-where-they-all-come-from' faction. (Remember that wherever fins stick up on the back or belly of a fish, bones will be found digging inwards.)

The size of the belly/rib cage cavity governs the number of perfect round cutlets that can be produced from a fish, i.e. those which can be cut below the vent. Hake, cod and monkfish have a long tail-end, while mullet are much shorter. Salmon compensates by having quite a thick layer of flesh around the belly side, but bass is a financial disaster as only the top half has meat on it. (Avoid a plump-bellied bass, as it's probably swallowed a mackerel or herring whole and you are paying bass prices for half-digested inferior dead fish!)

## COOKING WHOLE ROUND FISH

A fish kettle is very useful for poaching, but the old-fashioned way of wrapping the whole fish in wet newspaper (see page 14) is even more effective. While the use of flavoured salted water or court-bouillon (page 184) to give poached fish that 'je ne sais quoi' was until recently very popular, it definitely alters the flavour and is this really what one wants if the fish is in good condition? I think the flavour of the fish should be allowed to speak for itself.

MONKFISH – *Another ugly fish, and only the tail is sold. Very firm flesh does not flake so is excellent for skewering. Mild flavour, no bones and no scales. Good value, although expensive. Very high ratio of flesh to bone.*

GREY MULLET – *Medium-sized fish usually of good and interesting flavour, although some can be muddy-tasting. Soft texture. Scales and some large bones. Usually cooked whole, but can be filleted.*

RED MULLET – *Very distinctive flavour, loses its large scales very easily and is often seen with damaged bellies due to rough handling. Liver is highly prized. Can be bright orange, due to feeding. Some bones.*

RAINBOW TROUT – *Very popular, easily cooked (and overcooked!). Often farmed. Convenient size, whole fish for individual portions can be bought, also in fillets. Scales and some bones.*

SALMON – *Beautiful pink flesh which can be oily from farmed fish. Wild in season from February to the beginning of September. Sold whole, filleted or in cutlets. Good value. Medium-priced due to farming. Scales.*

SEA OR SALMON TROUT – *Very delicate flesh with delicious flavour. Medium/large fish, best cooked whole. Expensive, but well worth it. Not easily available. Scales and some fine bones.*

SEA BREAM – *Oval fish which is often sold filleted. Reddish skin. Delicate flavour and flakes easily. Not expensive. Scales.*

TUNA – *Very large fish. The flesh is so dark that it looks like animal meat. Good firm, meaty flesh, often sold in cutlets. Very dry if overcooked. Eaten raw, when cut like smoked salmon, by the Japanese.*

# Poached Cutlets with Hollandaise Sauce

OPTIONS

*Brill, cod, halibut, salmon, turbot*

6 fish cutlets,
each weighing about 200g/7oz

3.5 litres/6 pints court-bouillon
(page 184) or water

salt

350ml/12fl oz hollandaise sauce
(page 184), to serve

*This is the simplest dish in the world and, a bit like boiling an egg perfectly every time, one of the hardest to do well. Here it is served with hollandaise, one of the most famous of sauces.*

*I would describe it as butter thickened with egg yolks and variously flavoured. Some people add plain lemon juice, which I agree makes a delicious sauce, but not a true hollandaise and not nearly as good if you are going to serve a really good wine with it. That's why cooks go to the trouble of making a flavouring called a 'gastrique' (reduced wine, shallots and peppercorns), which flavours the butter and eggs divinely (see page 185).*

*If your fish is turbot or salmon, or any of the well-flavoured ones, poach it in salted water. If, however, it is one that could do with a bit more added flavour, use a court-bouillon (page 184).*

Bring the court-bouillon or water to the boil (in 2 separate pans if you haven't a big enough one to fit the cutlets all in on a single layer). Add salt, remove from the heat, lower the cutlets into the water and allow them to heat through to the centre. You can tell when they're done as the centre bone will come away free from the flesh, like pulling a stalk from a ripe pear.

Take out of the water and remove the skin and the bone. Dry the fish on kitchen paper, place on individual plates and serve with the hollandaise sauce.

An afterthought: If you are using a deep saucepan, it's an idea to line it with a tea towel or a long piece of foil. Then you can lift out the cutlets much more easily.

# Poached Fish in Green Parsley Sauce

*This is a very British dish, but the sauce is quite surprising in that the parsley when puréed gives off a brilliant green juice which adds both a vivid colour and flavour.*

Tear the leaves off the parsley stalks and crush the stalks with a meat mallet. Place them in a pan with the milk. Add the fish and bring up to boiling point. Poach gently until firm. Immediately remove the fish with a slotted spoon and set aside in a warm place.

Remove the parsley stalks from the milk and pour it into a blender. Add the parsley leaves and liquidize until the milk is bright green and the parsley leaves are chopped. With the machine still running, pour in the melted butter and add the flour. Empty it all into a saucepan and bring to the boil quickly.

Season the sauce and pour it over the fish, which has been arranged on a warmed serving dish. Quartered hard-boiled eggs make a good addition or decoration.

OPTIONS
*Cod, haddock,
halibut, turbot*

900g/2lb fish on the bone, filleted or in cutlets

125g/4½oz parsley

575ml/1 pint milk

85g/3oz butter, melted

50g/2oz flour

salt and freshly ground black pepper

3 hard-boiled eggs, quartered, to serve

# Mediterranean Fish Soup

large pinch of saffron
threads for colour

150ml/¼ pint boiling water

3 tablespoons olive oil

175g/6oz onions, chopped

4 garlic cloves, chopped

175g/6oz celery, chopped

450g/1lb tomatoes, chopped

175g/6oz leeks, chopped

175g/6oz bulb fennel,
trimmed and chopped

½ red sweet pepper,
deseeded and chopped

bay leaf

6 sprigs of tarragon

1 teaspoon dried thyme

small bunch of parsley

150ml/¼ pint white wine

about 1.75 litres/3 pints fish stock
(page 183)

salt and freshly ground black pepper

*You can't make a good fish soup without a good fish stock. See page 183 for advice on preparing and storing stocks.*
*To make the soup into a main course, poach some pieces of filleted fish in it. A bit of lobster (if you have any lying around) lifts it into the Glamorous Soup league....*

In a small bowl, put the saffron to soak in the boiling water.

Heat the oil in a large heavy-based pan and cook the onion, garlic, celery, tomatoes, leeks, fennel and peeled pepper until they are brown and pulpy. This takes quite a long time because the tomatoes hold a lot of water.

Add the herbs. Then add the wine and boil it away. Add the saffron with its liquid, half the stock to cover and simmer for half an hour at least, topping up with more of the stock as necessary.

Blend the mixture in a liquidizer until smooth, thin out with the rest of the stock and season with salt and lots of pepper. There should by now be about 1.25 litres/2¼ pints of liquid.

Pour it into deep warmed bowls and serve with crusty bread.

# Chilled Fish Vichyssoise

*Sometimes fish stock on its own in a soup is rather lacking in depth of flavour, especially when served cold. Adding some fresh chicken stock works wonders, or you could use a strong vegetable stock if you are serving vegetarians.*

Simmer the stocks together to reduce them to about 575 ml/1 pint and produce a more concentrated flavour.

Sweat the leeks and potatoes in one-third of the butter for 5 minutes but do not allow to brown. Add water to cover and simmer until the potatoes are tender.

Liquidize the potato and leek mixture until smooth, adding some of the mixed stock as necessary to keep the mixture fluid enough to allow the machine to turn.

Return the purée to the saucepan and mix in the rest of the stock. Season with salt and plenty of pepper and bring to the boil.

Put a ladleful of the hot liquid into the liquidizer, add the rest of the butter and an egg yolk, cover and blend at top speed.

Now whisk this into the soup in the saucepan.

Chill to serve cold and garnish with a few cooked prawns or shrimps together with a sprinkling of chopped spring onions.

1.1 litres/2 pints fish stock (page 183)

575 ml/1 pint chicken stock (see left)

450g/1lb leeks, sliced

175g/6oz butter

225g/½lb potatoes

1 egg yolk

salt and freshly ground black pepper

few peeled cooked shrimps or prawns, to garnish

greens of 1 or 2 spring onions, sliced into rings, to garnish

# Saffron Soup

OPTIONS
*Lobster, cod, coley, dogfish,*
*ling, monkfish, shark*

large pinch of saffron strands

150ml/¼ pint boiling water

4 tomatoes

1 tablespoon olive oil

2 garlic cloves, sliced

pinch of dried thyme

2-3 sprigs of tarragon

bay leaf

1.1 litres/2 pints light fish stock
(page 183)

2 teaspoons flour

30g/1oz butter

1 small tub (250ml/8fl oz)
crème fraîche

1 cooked lobster (see pages 104-5),
broken into pieces, or a few pieces
of cooked fish (about 225g/8oz),
cut into pieces

salt and freshly ground black pepper

greens of 1 or 2 spring onions,
sliced into rings, to garnish

*This is a beautiful soup with a fine flavour. Add some more fish or shellfish and a few cooked potatoes, and it becomes a meal in itself. You can be as extravagant or as parsimonious as you please, using lobster for that special occasion as here, or sticking to everyday fish, such as cod, for a family supper.*

In a bowl, infuse the saffron in the boiling water for 10 minutes.

Skin and deseed the tomatoes. Put them in a deep heavy-based saucepan with the oil and garlic. Add the thyme, tarragon and bay leaf and cook over a high heat, pulping the tomatoes down. Add half the fish stock. Blend the butter with the flour and whisk it in. Bring to the boil, thin out with the saffron water and remove the bay leaf.

Liquidize the soup and return it to the pan with the rest of the stock. Mix well and season. Whisk in the crème fraîche and bring to the boil. Heat the lobster or fish pieces in it until the flesh is just warmed through.

Serve garnished with some rings of spring onion greens.

# Chilled Smoked Fish, Coconut and Tarragon Soup

OPTIONS
*Smoked cod, smoked haddock, golden cutlets*

450g/1lb smoked fish

2 tablespoons grapeseed or groundnut oil

2 shallots, finely chopped

150ml/¼ pint tarragon vinegar

150ml/¼ pint white wine

300ml/½ pint fish stock

3 (400ml/14fl oz) tins of coconut milk

2 teaspoons chopped tarragon

salt and freshly ground black pepper

chopped chives, to garnish

salmon eggs, to garnish (optional)

*I am often asked what can be used as a substitute for cream. Obviously, whatever is used, the results won't be quite the same, but that is not to say that it won't be delicious. So why not try using tinned coconut milk instead? It usually works quite well, even in white sauces.*

Put the oil and shallots in a large saucepan with the vinegar and white wine and simmer gently to reduce the liquid until it has almost all gone.

Add the fish stock, bring to the boil and simmer for 10 minutes until the tarragon and wine flavour has been released from the shallots.

Put the pieces of smoked fish in the pan and poach them lightly in the stock for 2 minutes. Add the coconut milk and tarragon, bring to the boil and switch off the heat. Allow the soup to cool and then chill it.

Chill the soup bowls and divide the soup and the fish pieces between them. Adjust the seasoning. Sprinkle with chopped chives and add some salmon eggs for that special occasion.

# Oven-cooked Cutlets with Thyme and Lemon

*One of my favourite recipes, this dish is so easy to adapt to any kind of fish cutlets, fillets or whatever. Originally we made it with hake and a version was shown on Keith Floyd's first television programme.*

Preheat the oven to 190°C/375°F/gas5.

Gently simmer the onions, garlic, bay, thyme and peppercorns in 85g/3oz of the butter. Do not allow to brown.

Season the cutlets. Spread the onion mix in the bottom of an ovenproof dish and lay the fish on top. Put on top of each cutlet a knob of the remaining butter, a good grating of fresh nutmeg and the lemon slices. Tuck the potato pieces around, cover everything with foil and bake in the oven for 35 minutes.

When the fish is cooked (the centre bone will come out readily), pour off the juices into a small pan and reduce them to a concentrated buttery sauce.

Remove any bones and skin from the cutlets, pour the sauce back over them and serve. For a special dinner, coat with plenty of thick hollandaise sauce (page 184) before serving.

OPTIONS
*Cod, hake*

6 fish cutlets,
each weighing about 175g/6oz

2 onions, chopped

2 garlic cloves, crushed

2 bay leaves

1 teaspoon fresh lemon thyme leaves

6 black peppercorns

115g/4oz butter

2 potatoes, parboiled in salted water and cut into walnut-sized pieces

freshly grated nutmeg to taste

6 lemon slices

# Baked Fish with Gooseberry Sauce

*This sauce is usually prepared to accompany grilled mackerel — but it is lovely with any fish, oily or not. Use cooking gooseberries that are still tart. (You can also substitute cooking apples for an apple sauce!)*

Preheat the oven to 230°C/450°F/gas3.

Season the steaks, reform them into a fish shape and wrap them together (or wrap each of the whole fish individually), first in wet greaseproof paper and then in 6 thicknesses of wet newspaper. Either way, bake in the hot oven for 20 minutes.

Remove from the oven and unroll the fish from the paper wrappings. Remove any skin or loose bones and brush with a little melted butter.

Meanwhile, simmer the gooseberries in a couple of teaspoons of water with a little sugar to taste, until soft. Purée them in a blender or food processor while still hot, then add the remaining butter, cut into pieces. Finally add the egg yolks.

Plate the fish with a little sauce on the side, passing the rest in a sauce boat. Serve with buttered new potatoes.

OPTIONS

*Bass (pictured), cod, hoki, salmon*

6 fish steaks, each weighing about 175g/6oz or 6 small whole fish, each weighing about 350g/12oz

225g/8oz butter

225g/8oz fresh gooseberries

sugar to taste

2 egg yolks

salt and freshly ground black pepper

# Baked Fish in a Salt Crust

OPTIONS
*Bass, large rainbow trout,
salmon, sea trout*

1 whole fish,
weighing about 3.25kg/7lb,
cleaned

5 or 6 leaves from a fennel bulb
or stalks of lemon grass

900g/2lb plain flour

900g/2lb coarse sea salt

cold crème fraîche, to serve

*This is a useful technique for preparing hot food for picnics, buffets or party dinners. The appearance of the dish is not flattering but the flavour more than makes up for it. The trick is to get the flour mixture to the right consistency, like that of stiff porridge: too much water and the coating slides off the fish; too little and it won't spread. So have some extra flour and water handy to adjust the mixture.*

Preheat the oven to 250°C/475°F/gas9. Put aside a couple of handfuls of the salt for under the fish.

In a large bowl, mix together the remaining salt and the flour. Then mix in 900ml/1½ pints of water. Add some more water, a little at a time, until the correct consistency is achieved (that of stiff porridge, see introduction above).

Sprinkle the salt in a line on a large baking sheet, place the prepared fish on this and slap the flour-and-salt coating on top until everything is covered (but NOT underneath).

Immediately put to bake in the very hot oven and cook until set and dry (about 35 minutes for a fish of this size).

Remove from the oven and allow to rest for at least 20 minutes before tackling. From the tail end first and working upwards, peel off the crust (as well as any skin that does not come away with the crust) and discard.

Lift portions of the cooked fish gently from the bones on to warmed plates. Serve cold crème fraîche separately.

# Braised Fennel and Fish Steaks or Paupiettes

*Some fish, like monkfish, release a lot of liquid as they cook; whereas others, like halibut, stay firm and dry. So watch the fish and compensate accordingly while they are cooking, by adding a little water or stock.*

In a wide pan, place the fennel, butter and enough water to come halfway up the vegetable. Season very lightly. Cover, bring just to the boil and simmer until the fennel is nearly cooked.

Remove the lid, turn the fennel over, raise the heat and boil off the water. Fry the fennel until it takes on a little colour (a non-stick pan helps enormously at this point). Remove the fennel from the pan, add the seasoned fish and herbs and allow them to stiffen in the butter on both sides. Season.

Cover and braise the fish for 15 minutes or until the bone in the centre can be removed readily. For rolled fillets, you will only need about 5 or 6 minutes.

Return the fennel to the pan, baste with the lemon juice mix (if it is looking a little dry, add a little fish stock as well).

Sprinkle with chopped parsley to serve.

OPTIONS

*Halibut, monkfish, cod, turbot, rolled skinned fillets of brill, sole, haddock*

6 fish steaks or skinned fillets rolled as paupiettes, each weighing about 175g/6oz

2 large fennel bulbs, each cut into 6 wedges through the base

115g/4oz butter

2 teaspoons lemon juice mixed with 2 tablespoons water

2 tablespoon fish stock (optional, see page 183)

salt and freshly ground black pepper

1 tablespoon chopped parsley, to garnish

# Fish in Foil with Lemon and Herbs

OPTIONS
*Bass, parrot fish, trout, salmon, sea trout*

*The cooking juices that gather when the fish is buttered and wrapped in foil can be made into, or added to, a sauce if the fish and sauce are to be served hot. However, the butter becomes greasy when cold; so if the fish is to be served cold, it should be brushed with oil and a separate cold sauce be made independently.*

1 whole fish, weighing about 3.25kg/7lb (or 2 or 3 smaller whole fish about the same total weight)

fine salt

few sprigs of herbs, such as tarragon, parsley and chervil, plus 2 tablespoons of the herbs chopped

few black peppercorns

85g/3oz butter, melted (for hot fish only)

5 tablespoons grapeseed or groundnut oil (for hot or cold fish)

little lemon juice

Preheat the oven to 190°C/375°F/gas5.

Scale the fish if you wish to eat the skin, otherwise just season the inside with salt, sprinkling it evenly in the cavity. Tuck the whole herb sprigs in together with a few peppercorns.

Unroll a piece of strong foil a little more than either double the length or twice the thickness of the fish and generously spread it with some soft butter or brush with oil if serving cold. Sprinkle more salt evenly all over it. Place the fish on one half of the piece of foil and fold the other half over to form a loose package. Roll or fold up the edges to seal in the steam which forms inside the package as it cooks.

Lift the package on to a large baking sheet or upturned roasting tin and put it in the oven, positioning it diagonally if necessary to fit. Cook for 40 minutes, then allow it to rest for 2 minutes until the foil is cool enough to touch.

*This next bit is messy!* Slide the package on to a large dish which will catch the juices when the foil is removed. Slit the foil around the base of the fish, preferably with a pair of scissors, and ease out the foil from underneath the fish. Now remove the rest of the foil, clean off the skin and fin bones (also the darker flesh if you don't like it) and pour the juices off into a bowl.

If serving hot: slide the fish very carefully on to a warmed serving dish, cover with a fresh piece of foil and keep warm. Strain the juices in the bowl into a pan with the chopped herbs and remaining butter melted and acidulated with a little lemon juice. Heat gently, adjust the seasoning and serve the sauce separately.

If serving cold: remove the skin as above, but then allow the fish to become quite cold. Serve with mayonnaise (page 184) or, for a change, some chilled spicy Thai seafood soup base (page 110) which has been thickened by reducing it a little.

# Spicy Fillets in Foil

*This dish is basically Moroccan in style and although it has all the looks of something that is chilli-hot it actually has no heat, only lots of lovely spicy flavours.*

Preheat the oven to 200°C/400°F/gas6.

In a frying pan, mix together all the herbs and spices with the garlic and oil. Cook over a moderate heat for 2 minutes and add the fish stock. Boil down to a thick paste and season well.

Spread out a large piece of foil and lay the fillets on it, skin sides upwards. Spread the fish all over with the paste. Wrap the foil around the fish to form a loose but tightly sealed package. Place on a large baking sheet and bake for 30 minutes.

Unwrap and roll on to a warmed serving dish, with all the juices. Remove the skin if it has not been scaled.

Serve with couscous.

OPTIONS
*Bass, grey mullet, mackerel*

whole fillets from a 3.25kg/7lb fish or 175kg/4lb fish fillets

30g/1oz chopped parsley

2 tablespoons ground cumin

2 tablespoons paprika

1 garlic clove, crushed

6 tablespoons olive oil

300ml/½ pint fish stock (page 183), reduced by half

salt and freshly ground black pepper

73

# Brochettes with Fish Chunks and Bacon

OPTIONS
*Cod, halibut, monkfish, turbot*

1kg/2¼lb skinned fish fillets,
cut into cubes

150ml/¼ pint olive oil

juice of 1 lemon

150ml/¼ pint white wine

1 onion, grated

225g/8oz streaky bacon, each slice
cut across in half

about 18 fresh bay leaves

freshly ground black pepper

*One of the problems of skewering fish is that unless you use monkfish or swordfish, the flesh tends to break up into flakes and fall off. Rolling slices of bacon round the pieces of fish and then fixing it in place on the skewer usually solves this problem, as well as seasoning the fish.*

Boil together the oil, lemon, wine, onion and seasoning to taste for 5 minutes. Allow to cool. Leave the fish to marinate in this mixture for a couple of hours.

Remove the fish from the marinade and pat dry. Roll a piece of bacon around a chunk of fish and secure it by impaling it on a metal skewer. Continue in this way with the remaining slices of bacon and pieces of fish, sharing them between 6 skewers and impaling a bay leaf in between every other piece.

Place the skewers in a tray under a preheated hot grill and cook them, turning them and basting them with the marinade until they are firm and the bacon well cooked.

# Brioche Beignets

*These delicious deep-fried fishy beignets are wonderful for parties, or have them as a first course for a summer lunch. Either way, the fresh tomato coulis is an excellent accompaniment, as would be the chilli dipping sauce on page 135.*

Well ahead of time, make the brioche dough: mix the yeast and sugar with the warm water in a small bowl. Leave until frothy.

Then sift the flour and salt into a large bowl and add the butter. Rub it in with the fingers, then add the egg and the yeast mixture and beat well until it forms a smooth dough. Cover with a damp cloth and leave to rise until doubled in bulk. Beat down and leave to rise again until doubled again. Beat down again once more just before use.

Make the tomato coulis: simmer the tomatoes in hot oil with the garlic and sugar for 15 minutes, until soft. Sieve to remove the skin and pips. Season with salt and pepper. Keep warm.

Now make the beignets: season the fish, mix with the warmed brioche paste and roll the mixture into walnut-sized balls.

Coat the balls with breadcrumbs and deep-fry in hot oil in 2 or 3 batches for about 5 minutes each, until hazelnut brown. Drain each batch on paper towels and keep warm until all are cooked.

Serve immediately, with the tomato coulis.

OPTIONS
*Cod, haddock, hake, monkfish*

about 1kg/2¼lb boned and cooked fish

85g/3oz fresh or dried breadcrumbs

grapeseed or groundnut oil, for deep-frying

*for the brioche paste:*
200g/7oz strong flour

2 eggs

140g/5oz unsalted butter, diced

¼ teaspoon salt

3 tablespoons warm water

⅓ level teaspoon dry yeast

1 teaspoon sugar

*for the tomato coulis:*
about 675g/1½lb tomatoes, coarsely chopped

2 tablespoons grapeseed or groundnut oil

1 garlic clove, crushed

pinch of sugar

salt and freshly ground black pepper

# *Fish Cutlets with Crab Bisque Sauce*

OPTIONS
*Cod, hake, salmon*

6 fish cutlets

150ml/¼ pint grapeseed or
groundnut oil

3 medium onions, sliced

3 carrots, sliced

6 tomatoes, sliced

1 teaspoon dried thyme

6 black peppercorns

3 bay leaves

150ml/¼ pint white wine

150ml/¼ pint fish stock (page 183)

115g/4oz butter

6 or 9 cooked crab claws

*Fresh crab meat has a very strong flavour which here transforms the braised vegetables into a delicious 'coulis'. The crab shell cooked in with the fish stock also increases the flavour.*

In a large frying pan, heat the oil and brown the sliced onions in it until they take on a good dark colour. Add the carrots, tomatoes, thyme, peppercorns and bay leaves. Simmer everything together until the vegetables have softened. Add the white wine and boil it down until it has nearly all gone. Then add the stock, season with salt and bring to the boil.

Lay the fish cutlets on top of the vegetables, cover and simmer gently for 15 minutes. Meanwhile, remove the meat from the crab claws and set aside.

Lift the fish out of the pan and remove any unwanted bones and skin. Keep warm on a warmed serving plate.

Now strain the vegetables through a sieve, passing as much pulp as will easily go through. If there is too much liquid, boil this off until a smooth pulp is achieved. Remove from the heat. Whisk in the butter, add the crab meat and adjust the seasoning, especially the pepper. Reheat but do not allow to boil.

Lift out some of the crab meat from the sauce with a slotted spoon and pile it on top of the cutlets. Pour the rest of the sauce over and around to serve.

# Fish Cutlets with Fennel, Garlic and Flageolets Verts

*Thanks to the inestimable Rick Stein, it has become very fashionable to serve beans with fish. With lots of stock and a bit of bacon the result might even be described as 'chowder'. Cooking beans this way, they are really only an alternative to potato or bread, serving to mop up the juices. Green ones don't need anything exotic to render them appetizing, unlike, say, white ones.*

In a large heavy-based saucepan, fry the onions gently in the butter until softened. Add the diced carrots, fennel, garlic and thyme. Cover with water and simmer for 8 minutes.

Add half the fish stock and cook until the vegetables are tender. Crush the garlic into the pan and discard the skin. Add the flageolets verts. Season.

Meanwhile in a large saucepan, reduce the Noilly Prat to one-third of its original volume and add the rest of the fish stock. Place the cutlets in this, cover and simmer for up to 20 minutes, or until the centre bones will lift out easily. Remove the skin.

Arrange the beans on a flat warmed serving dish and tuck the cutlets among them. Pour the juices over and serve.

OPTIONS
*Cod, hake, monkfish, salmon*

6 fish cutlets,
each weighing about 170g/6oz

3 onions, sliced

115g/4oz butter

2 carrots, diced

1 small fennel bulb, trimmed
and cut into 3 wedges, with the
leaves separated

1 whole garlic clove (or more!)

½ teaspoon dried thyme

300ml/½ pint fish stock (page 183)

2 large (400g/14oz) tins
of flageolets verts

300ml/½ pint Noilly Prat
white vermouth

salt and freshly ground black pepper

# Fish Balls with Chilli and Tomato Sauce

OPTIONS
*Cod, coley, haddock, hake*

450g/1lb flaked cooked fish

115g/4oz onions, chopped

15g/½oz ginger, peeled and grated

1 garlic clove, crushed

3 eggs

30g/1oz flour, plus more for dusting

grapeseed or groundnut oil,
for deep-frying

*for the chilli and tomato sauce:*
1½ tablespoons grapeseed or
groundnut oil

2 onions, finely chopped

450g/1lb tomatoes,
skinned and deseeded

2 teaspoons tomato paste

2 garlic cloves, crushed

2.5cm/1in piece of root ginger,
peeled and grated

3 fresh chillies

115g/4oz butter

1 teaspoon chopped fresh thyme

salt and freshly ground black pepper

*Any leftover white fish that flakes can be used to make these flavourful treats. The sauce is also useful for pepping up any dish made with blander fish.*

First make the sauce: heat the oil in a frying pan and fry the onions and tomatoes until softened. Add the tomato paste, ground garlic, ginger and chilli. Moisten with 150ml/¼ pint water. Beat in the butter and herbs. Simmer for about 10 minutes. Adjust the seasoning and keep warm.

To make the fish balls: in a bowl, mix together the onions, ginger, garlic and cooked fish. Add the eggs and the flour and mix well. Season the mixture well.

Roll the mixture into 'golf-balls'. Dust these with more flour and deep-fry the fish balls in hot oil in 2 or 3 batches until golden. Drain each batch on paper towels and keep warm while the rest are being cooked.

Serve piled up in a warmed serving dish with the sauce poured over them.

# Spiced Lentil Fish Cakes

*The first time I cooked this dish I had made a dhall with Egyptian lentils and had some left over. By adding some flaked fish and a couple of eggs these 'cakes' were a wonderful find. You must dry out the dhall first, though, and make it thick. I found a few minutes in the microwave cooker on high was the best way of drying the lentils, as the liquid evaporated without the lentils sticking and burning. Failing that, a non-stick pan is almost as good.*

Cook the onions, garlic, chilli and spices in oil for a few minutes until aromatic. Add the lentils and fry for a few minutes more, then add just enough water to cover. Simmer until the lentils are completely tender and the water has been absorbed.

Purée the mixture in a blender or food processor and then dry it out, either in the microwave (see introduction above) or in a non-stick pan over a moderate heat, stirring all the time. The texture should be like that of mashed potato.

Now, off the heat, add the eggs and mix in well. Flake the fish and mix it in. Season well. Allow to cool, then shape into cakes to fry or just drop large spoonfuls into a hot lightly oiled non-stick frying pan, moulding them into cakes. Cook until firm, turn and cook until golden on both sides.

Serve with raw onion rings and cold sliced tomatoes.

OPTIONS
*Cod, haddock, hake, mackerel, salmon, turbot*

225g/8oz (or more) flaked cooked fish (not smoked)

2 onions, chopped

2 garlic cloves, crushed

2 green chillies, sliced

2 teaspoons turmeric

1 tablespoon ground coriander seeds

2 teaspoons ground ginger

2 tablespoons grapeseed or groundnut oil

115g/4oz lentils rinsed

2 eggs

salt and freshly ground black pepper

# Fish Cakes

OPTIONS

*Cod, bream, coley, haddock, smoked haddock, hake, mackerel, salmon (pictured), tilapia*

225g/8oz cooked fish, broken up and skin and bones removed

450g/1lb freshly cooked potato

85g/3oz butter, plus more for frying (optional)

1 tablespoon chopped parsley

50g/2oz fresh breadcrumbs

2 eggs

salt and freshly ground black pepper

grapeseed or groundnut oil, for frying (optional)

*The whole secret of fish cakes that are fit for the Gods lies in making delicious mashed potato that holds together – and that means lots of butter. The chopped parsley gives a fresh 'spring-like' flavour.*

Mash the potato, season with salt and pepper and add the butter and parsley while the potatoes are still hot. Mix well and adjust the seasoning if necessary.

Add the fish and mix it in gently so as not to mash it as well. Roll the mixture into a long sausage shape and cut this into 12 pieces. Form these into cakes.

Put the eggs in one shallow dish and the breadcrumbs in another. Dip each cake first in flour, then in the egg and finally in the flour again, shaking off any excess each time. Fry the cakes in hot oil (or better still, butter for a little extra cholesterol...) until well browned on both sides.

Serve with a sharply dressed herby green salad.

# Breadcrumb Fish Cakes

OPTIONS
*Cod, haddock, hake*

175g/6oz fresh breadcrumbs

225g/8oz flaked cooked fish

1 onion, finely chopped

1 tablespoon finely chopped parsley

3 eggs

50g/2oz butter

little milk (optional)

salt and freshly ground black pepper

butter or grapeseed or
groundnut oil, for frying

*The English have always been happy to use breadcrumbs for stuffing – and here we do just that, but turn it into a breakfast dish with the fish in the stuffing instead of the other way round.*

Mix 115g/4oz of the crumbs with the fish, onion and parsley. Bind with 1 of the eggs. Melt the butter and add it, together with a little milk if the mixture still seems dry. Season the mixture and mould it into cakes.

Put the other 2 eggs in a shallow bowl and beat lightly. Put the remaining breadcrumbs in another similar bowl. Coat the cakes first with the egg and then breadcrumbs, shaking off excess each time and fry in hot butter or oil until they are golden brown on both sides, turning once.

Eat with crisp streaky bacon for breakfast.

# Fish Quiche

*I am really not sure if 'quiche' is the right term for this dish, perhaps a better description is 'open tart', as the filling is quite a fluid sauce rather than a set custard.*

In a large, heavy-based pan, simmer the shallots in the vermouth for 5 minutes, then allow them to cool. Lay the fish in the cooled mixture and leave the fillets to marinate for about 1 hour, turning them from time to time.

Poach the fish gently in the mixture until the flesh is firm, about 5 minutes. Strain and retain the liquid. Allow the fish to continue to drain and cool with the shallots and then flake it or roughly break it up.

Preheat a hot grill.

In a saucepan, make a roux by melting the butter and stirring in the flour, then cooking the mixture for a couple of minutes. Measure the drained liquid, top it up to 300ml/½ pint with some of the milk, then beat it into the roux. Bring to the boil and cook for several minutes, stirring continuously, until thick and smooth.

Add the mustard, nutmeg and cream, together with any extra liquid from the fish. Adjust the seasoning and consistency, which will probably have thinned out a bit when the fish was added, but add more milk if necessary – aim for thick pouring consistency. Fold in the fish and turn the mixture into the pastry case.

Sprinkle with cheese and brown under the grill to serve.

OPTIONS
*Halibut, monkfish, cod, turbot, rolled skinned fillets of brill, sole, haddock*

675g/1½lb filleted fish, preferably skinned

4 shallots, chopped

300ml/½ pint Noilly Prat white vermouth

75g/2½oz butter

50g/2oz flour

about 150ml/¼ pint milk

2 teaspoons mustard

freshly grated nutmeg to taste

5 tablespoons double cream

1 medium (25cm/10in) shortcrust pastry shell, baked blind (see page 52)

30g/1oz Cheddar cheese, grated

salt and freshly ground black pepper

# Smoked Fish Scrambled Egg and Courgettes Ribbons on Rösti

*Smoked salmon and creamy scrambled eggs really are a special-occasion breakfast — the sort of thing you have in glamorous hotels. In that form they aren't really substantial enough for a lunch dish, or even a first course. Set them on rösti and top them with glistening green and gold ribbons of stir-fried courgettes and they immediately qualify for this more exalted position.*

*Use whatever kind of smoked fish is most readily available, but be sure to use undyed fish and take care when adding salt to the scrambled eggs because some smoked fish is very salty indeed.*

Cook the fish (unless it is smoked halibut, salmon or trout) in a little water until it flakes. Remove bones and skin, and flake it.

Peel the potatoes and grate them raw. Drain through a sieve into a bowl, squeezing out as much liquid as possible by taking handfuls in your fists. Allow the liquid to settle for a minute and then pour it off, leaving the starch granules behind in the bowl.

Add the grated potato to the bowl. Season and add the spring onions or chives. Add the cornflour and mix well.

Heat some oil for frying in a large frying pan (or two smaller ones). Divide the mixture into 6 balls, flatten them into cakes and press down into the oil. Allow the cakes to brown over a moderate heat for about 5 minutes on each side. They should now be cooked through. Transfer to a large warmed serving plate and keep warm.

Slice the courgettes lengthwise with a potato peeler or a mandolin grater and fry these shreds lightly for a minute or two in half the butter, turning them several times. Season them.

Melt the remaining butter in another large heavy-based saucepan over a gentle heat. Add the eggs and stir continuously until scrambled to taste, adding seasoning and the flaked cooked fish just before they have reached your preferred consistency.

Turn the eggs out on to the potato cakes and pile the courgette strips on top. Garnish with more spring onions or chives and serve.

### OPTIONS

*Smoked cod, smoked haddock (pictured), golden cutlets, smoked halibut, smoked salmon, smoked trout*

675g/1½lb smoked fish

450g/1lb potatoes

2 tablespoons chopped spring onion greens or chopped chives, plus more to garnish

1 teaspoon cornflour

675g/1½lb courgettes

115g/4oz butter

12-18 eggs

grapeseed or groundnut oil, for frying

salt and freshly ground black pepper

# Fish in Sour Cream Sauce

OPTIONS
*Any fish*

6 fish steaks,
each weighing about 170g/6oz

12 baby carrots

2 yellow courgettes, sliced

50g/2oz butter

3 tablespoons grapeseed or
groundnut oil

1 onion, chopped

½ red sweet pepper,
deseeded and chopped

150ml/¼ pint fish stock (page 183)

½ tablespoon chopped tarragon

1 small tub (250ml/8fl oz)
sour cream or crème fraîche

125g/4½oz spinach

salt and freshly ground black pepper

*Using sour cream eliminates the need for using any other souring agent in the sauce – a useful tip if you don't want to buy wine – but the resulting flavour is a lot less sophisticated and the interest has to be introduced by means of the addition of some fresh vegetables and herbs.*

In boiling salted water, parboil the carrots. Sear the courgettes in a little butter. Set both aside.

In a large pan, heat the butter and oil together over a fairly high heat. Stiffen the pieces of fish in this and lift out of the pan.

Fry the chopped onion and red pepper gently in the pan until they soften. Pour in the fish stock and boil to reduce to half the amount. Add the tarragon with the cream and bring to the boil.

Return the fish to the pan with the spinach, courgettes and carrots. Simmer everything together gently for 5 minutes, adding some water if it becomes too dry. Season with plenty of pepper and a little salt if necessary.

# Spiced Fish Steaks with Chilli Hot Sauce

*The coconut milk will thicken, as double cream would, while you cook the fish. If it doesn't thicken sufficiently to give a coating consistency in the time, to avoid overcooking the fish you may need to pour some of it off and boil it down in a separate pan. Although chilli lovers may be able to enjoy an authentic chilli hot sauce, mere mortals like me prefer diluting it considerably with sour cream and then I can eat it by the bucketful.*

Put the oil in a frying pan over a high heat and sear the outside of the fish in it. Remove.

Add the onions, garlic and turmeric with water to cover. Cook until the water is boiled off and they fry lightly together. Return the fish to the pan. Add the ginger, cinnamon stick, coconut milk and stock. Cover and simmer for 3-4 minutes for fillets, 7-8 for steaks, turning the fish once and reducing the sauce to a coating consistency. Season.

While the fish is cooking, make the chilli hot sauce: in a blender, purée the chillies with the lemon zest and juice, and the oil. Season with to taste salt and pepper. If this is too hot for you, stir a couple of teaspoonfuls or more of it into a tub of soured cream to dilute it.

Serve the fish and its sauce on individual warmed plates with boiled yellow-fleshed sweet potatoes and the chilli hot sauce served separately.

OPTIONS
*Any fish*

6 fish steaks or folded skinned fillets, each weighing about 175g/6oz

2 tablespoons grapeseed or groundnut oil

100g/3½oz onions, chopped

4 garlic cloves, crushed

45g/1½oz ground turmeric

50g/2oz grated root ginger

1 cinnamon stick

575ml/1 pint coconut milk

125ml/4 fl oz fish stock (page 183)

salt and freshly ground black pepper

*for the chilli hot sauce:*
3 chillies

zest and juice of 2 lemons

3 tablespoons olive oil

small tub (250ml/8fl oz) of sour cream (optional)

# Gigot of Monkfish with Saffron Niçoise

*This is best made with a monkfish tail as it is so easy to skin whole, but any round fish can be cooked in a similar way, until the skin will peel off, and then basting it with the Niçoise mixture.*

Soak the saffron in 150ml/¼ pint of water, preferably overnight. Then bring to the boil and simmer for 5 minutes.

Preheat the oven to 220°C/425°F/gas7. In a saucepan, stew the tomatoes with the garlic in the oil until soft. Add the wine and boil rapidly until the mixture is just a pulp again. Add the stock and saffron with its water, the herbs and seasoning.

Skin the monkfish and remove its flabby membranes. Shorten the tail with scissors, but do not cut into the flesh or it will shrink back and expose the bone while it cooks. If using whole fish, leave the skin on and oil it.

Bake in the hot oven for 30 minutes, until the flesh pulls away from the bone readily. Baste frequently with the saffron mixture. If using whole fish, take it out after 20 minutes to peel the skin off and then start basting from that point.

If an excess of liquid has oozed from the fish, pour off the saffron sauce, boil it down a little and when the fish is dished up, pour it over and around, garnishing with some stoned black olives and fennel fronds.

OPTIONS
*Bass, cod, hake,
monkfish (pictured)*

1 monkfish tail,
weighing about 1.25kg/2½lb,
or 1.8kg/4lb fish, or 6 large cutlets

1 (5g) packet of saffron threads

6 medium tomatoes,
skinned and deseeded

2-3 garlic cloves, crushed

4 tablespoons olive oil,
plus more for brushing the fish

150ml/¼ pint white wine

300ml/½ pint fish stock
(page 183)

pinch of dried thyme

2-3 sprigs of tarragon

large pinch of dried sage

bay leaf

salt and freshly ground black pepper

18 black stoned olives,
to garnish

fennel fronds,
to garnish

# Stuffed Fish Steaks with Fresh Tomato Sauce

OPTIONS
*Bass, monkfish, salmon,
swordfish, tuna*

6 thick fish steaks,
each weighing about 175g/6oz

175g/6oz Cheddar cheese

6 pieces of smoked salmon,
about 10cm/4in long

55g/2oz butter

salt and freshly ground black pepper

*for the fresh tomato sauce:*
30g/1oz butter

1 onion, chopped

1 garlic clove, crushed

4 tomatoes, deseeded and whizzed
to a purée in a blender

150 ml/¼ pint fish stock
(page 183)

2 teaspoons tomato paste

½ tablespoon fresh marjoram,
plus more to garnish

½ teaspoon dried thyme

*If you don't want to use an expensive ingredient like smoked salmon, an applewood-smoked cheese in the stuffing can give some of the effect. Cook the fish just long enough to give the cheese time to melt and ooze deliciously from the pocket. The fish needs to be one that won't flake to pieces when it is cooked, so use a firm-fleshed type as specified.*

Cut a deep slit in the sides of each of the fish fillets to make a deep pocket, being careful not to tear the flesh and make a hole.

Cut the cheese into 6 oblongs and wrap them with the smoked salmon. Place these in the pockets of the fillets and stick a toothpick in to hold the fish closed. Season.

Melt the butter in a large frying pan over a high heat and lightly stiffen the fish in it.

In another pan, make the sauce: cook together the butter, onion, garlic and fresh tomatoes for 5 minutes. Add the fish stock blended with the tomato paste and the herbs, bring to the boil and season to taste.

Pour this mixture over the fish and cook gently until the fish is firm and the cheese starts to run.

Sprinkle with a little chopped marjoram to serve.

90

# Fish Crostini

*Just an Italian appetiser – or even a bit more than that – these piquant little morsels are perfect with drinks. Alternatively you can leave the slices whole and serve them as snacks or as dinner-party first courses.*

Preheat the oven to 250°C/465°F/gas9.

Make a very stiff white sauce, first cooking together the flour in the melted butter for a minute or two to make a roux and then stirring in the fish stock. Simmer for about 5 minutes, stirring continuously, until smooth. Add the cheeses to the sauce. Season generously with pepper.

Cut the fish into small squares or flakes and add enough sauce to bind them; how much will depend on the wetness of the fish.

Toast the bread, spread the mixture on it and sprinkle with chopped marjoram. Cook in the oven until it has browned.

Remove the crusts and cut the crostini into fingers or squares.

1½ tins (140g/5oz) of sardines in oil, drained

¼ tin (15g/½oz) of anchovies in oil, drained, rinsed and patted dry

20g/¾oz flour

20g/¾oz butter

150ml/¼ pint fish stock (page 183)

50g/2oz Gruyère cheese, cubed

50g/2oz Parmesan cheese, grated

1 teaspoon chopped fresh marjoram

1 French baguette, cut into slices

freshly ground black pepper

# Pithiviers of Fish

OPTIONS
*Any fish*

.

550g/1¼lb mixed fish flesh
(free of skin and bone)

450g/1lb puff pastry

whites of 2-3 eggs,
plus 2 whole eggs

4 sprigs of tarragon

300ml/½ pint whipping cream

1 teaspoon anchovy essence
(optional)

cooked peas and diced carrots
(optional)

115g/4oz butter

1 teaspoon lemon juice

salt and freshly ground black pepper

*Little pies that are made upside down! You'll need a bowl with bulging sloping sides like a sugar bowl, holding about 200ml/⅓ pint, to mould the pies. It is very simple and a technique which lends itself to all kinds of different fillings.*

Cut 350g/12oz of fish into chunks the size of medium prawns and reserve. Chill the rest of the fish in the freezer for 10 minutes.

Roll out the pastry and cut 6 rounds large enough to fit inside the bowl (see above) and come up the sides to the top. Re-roll the pastry trimmings, if necessary, and cut 6 more smaller rounds, using the bowl edge as the cutter. Keep cold. To line the bowl with one of the larger rounds, you'll need to cut out and remove a wedge of pastry to make it line the bowl snugly, pinching the pastry together to join it securely and moistening the edge with a little water if they won't stick.

In a blender, liquidize the chilled fish with the whites of 2 eggs plus 1 of the whole eggs, salt, pepper and half the tarragon to make a speckled purée, adding the extra egg white if necessary to make it smooth. Pour in the cream and blend it in quickly. Finish by hand, pouring everything into a bowl and mixing gently (too much beating and the cream will turn to butter). A little anchovy essence may be added to point up the fish flavour.

Fold the reserved fish chunks into the purée. A few added peas or carrots cut into little squares will provide colour and texture. Adjust the seasoning if necessary.

Put one-sixth of the filling into the pastry-lined bowl and top with one of the small rounds moistened at the rim. Squeeze the edges of the pastry together to seal and turn the pie out upside down. Tidy up the rim and mark the top of the pastry with a cutter in sickle shapes. Brush with a wash made from the remaining egg, lightly beaten, and make a hole in the top. Repeat with the remaining pastry and filling to make 5 more pies.

Cook in the oven for 30 minutes, then remove from the oven. In a small pan melt the butter and add the lemon juice and the remaining tarragon, finely chopped. Pour a little of this into each pie through the holes to serve.

# A Quick Fish Salad

OPTIONS
*Bass, cod, grey mullet, haddock, hake, mackerel, parrot fish, pomfret, salmon, sea trout, tilapia*

675g/1½ lb poached smoked or plain fish, well flaked

2 teaspoons chopped parsley

1 teaspoon chopped tarragon

2 teaspoons capers

1 small shallot, finely chopped

salt and freshly ground black pepper

squares of toast, to serve

*for the vinaigrette:*
2 teaspoons sugar

1 tablespoon white wine vinegar

1 teaspoon Dijon mustard

5 tablespoons hazelnut oil

*This refreshing salad, which could almost be classed as a pâté, makes a great start to a meal. Alternatively you can serve it as dip, with strips of pitta bread, vegetable crudités or taco chips.*

First make the vinaigrette: stir the sugar into the vinegar until it is completely dissolved. Add the mustard, stir well and whisk in the oil gradually.

Fold the vinaigrette, chopped herbs, capers and shallot into the fish. Season.

Serve in a bowl with squares of toast.

# Avocado and Smoked Fish Salad

*Some smoked fish like cod and haddock still needs further cooking, whereas salmon, trout, halibut may usually be eaten as they are. It is interesting to mix both types of fish here and the dish provides a good means of using up leftovers should you have been serving a fish platter at some point. Remember to keep everything cold. Cold leftover cooked young broad beans go very nicely in it as well.*

Steam any raw smoked fish (see above) over simmering water until firm. Allow to cool. Flake into small pieces and chill.

Slice the other smoked fish (see above) into strips and chill.

In a bowl, mix the sour cream, chilli powder, mayonnaise and juice of half the lemon. Season with salt and pepper. Chill.

Peel the oranges, slice them into rounds and drain. Peel the avocados, stone and dice all but one half. Brush this with lemon juice to keep it from discolouring. Fold the avocado dice into the sauce with the flaked fish.

Arrange some lettuce leaves in a ring around the edge of a serving plate, then arrange the orange slices around that. Pile the avocado mix in the centre. Cut the reserved avocado half into slices, brush these with lemon juice and arrange on top. Sprinkle with the cheese.

OPTIONS
*Smoked cod, smoked haddock, smoked halibut, smoked mackerel, smoked salmon, smoked trout*

225g/8oz mixed smoked fish (see above)

150ml/¼ pint sour cream

pinch of chilli powder

3 tablespoons mayonnaise (see page 184, or use ready-made)

juice of 1 lemon

3 oranges

3 avocados

2 little gems or other lettuce

1 tablespoon grated Cheddar cheese

salt and freshly ground black pepper

# Fish Salad with Ginger Mayonnaise

OPTIONS

*Cod, smoked cod,
smoked haddock, monkfish,
halibut cutlets, turbot cutlets*

675g/1½lb fish,
skinned, poached and drained

400ml/14 fl oz grapeseed or
groundnut oil

50g/2oz fresh ginger,
peeled and grated

4 egg yolks

1 teaspoon Dijon mustard

½ teaspoon salt

2 dessert apples, cored and diced

2 celery stalks, strings removed
and cut into thick slices

6 small new potatoes, cooked,
peeled and sliced

*Making flavoured mayonnaises is an easy way of widening your repertoire of sauces. Start by putting the oil into the blender and then throwing in some tender herbs like basil or tarragon and whizz them up until the oil turns green or, as in this particular recipe, just peel and grate some fresh ginger and purée it with the oil you are going to use to make your mayonnaise, as below. With this technique you can design your own personal versions of flavoured mayonnaise.*

Put the oil and ginger in the liquidizer and blend well together.

In a bowl, beat the egg yolks with an electric beater, adding the mustard and salt until the egg yolks become pale. With the machine still running, incorporate the oil, a little at a time, to make a stiff emulsion.

Fold in the fish, apples, celery and potatoes. Adjust the seasoning and thin out the mixture with a little water if it is too thick (water thins, oil thickens).

Serve with a salad and some crusty bread

# Terrine of Mousseline

OPTIONS
*Cod, haddock, parrot fish,*
*rainbow trout, salmon*

675g/1½lb raw fish,
free of skin and bones

about 575ml/1 pint strong fish stock
(page 183)

quenelle mousseline mixture
(opposite)

salt and freshly ground black pepper

*The mixture used for making the quenelles opposite is called a 'mousseline' and this preparation can be used as a binding mixture for lightly poached and drained pieces of fish. They must be pre-cooked or they will give off their juices into the mousseline as it cooks and spoil the texture with too much extra liquid.*

Season the fish and poach it very gently in the stock until firm. Drain, retaining the stock for a sauce or another occasion, and pat the fish dry. Allow to cool.

Preheat the oven to 110°C/230°F/gas¼. Line a 23cm/9in terrine with film, mix the fish with the mousseline and arrange it in the terrine. Cover and cook in a bain-marie (or a deep roasting pan half-filled with boiling water) in the oven until totally set, about 1 hour. Test with a skewer to see of it is set all the way through to the centre: it should come out dry.

Either turn out by lifting the cling film, slice and serve hot; or allow to cool with a light weight on top, then turn out and serve cold, possibly with an avocado salad.

# Fish Quenelles

*The word 'quenelle' actually describes a dumpling shape, but it is usually linked to a fish mousse preparation. Every fish is made of protein which will cook hard — like an egg. Some have more water and some have more gelatine than others and some are more flavourful. All these considerations affect the quantities required when making a mousseline. It's a balancing act of flavour and texture. More protein is often added in the form of egg white, which doesn't help the taste but gives a smooth texture.*

*This is a basic recipe, but you must be prepared to vary the quantity of cream. The more you add, the lighter it gets, until it all falls apart — an irremediable disaster. So start with too much protein and test, then add more cream if you feel it can soften more. Another tip: only poach until the insides are lightly cooked; like a soufflé, a little soft bit inside makes for a more exotic effect.*

OPTIONS
*Bass, cod, haddock, hake, salmon*

225g/8oz raw fish flesh, free of skin and bones

whites of 6-8 eggs

250ml/8fl oz double cream

250ml/8fl oz whipping cream

salt

white wine sauce (page 20), to serve

Put the fish in a blender or food processor with the salt. Cover with half the egg whites and blend until smooth, adding more egg whites if the mixture will not turn freely at any point.

Turn into a large bowl and mix in both of the creams. Whisk until the mixture thickens slightly. Chill.

Put a large pan of salted water on to boil. Once boiling, reduce the heat until the water is barely trembling. Dip a tablespoon into the water and then use it to take a spoonful of the chilled mixture and roll it against the edge of the bowl to form an oval-shaped quenelle. Dip the spoonful of mixture briefly into the water and then tap it against the side of the pan, so the quenelle drops off into the water. Repeat, working quickly, until the mixture is used up.

Poach the quenelles for about 8 minutes, turning them over halfway through. They should have the consistency of poached eggs and be slightly soft inside. Drain on paper towels, arrange on warmed plates and spoon the sauce over to serve.

# shellfish

*The sweet and delicious flesh of shellfish generally requires very little cooking. The real skill lies mostly in buying the best and freshest of specimens, careful preparation and subtle use of added flavourings*

## TYPES OF SHELLFISH

Each type of shellfish has a strong personality. The flavour of fresh mussels could never be confused with that of oysters, let alone lobster. However, perhaps such comparisons under the umbrella of shellfish are unhelpful: lobsters are, in fact, crustaceans, like crab and crayfish, and have firm fibrous flesh; whereas mussels are molluscs, like clams and scallops, and consist really of one rather soft muscle prone to overcooking.

## PREPARING AND COOKING SHELLFISH

As shellfish do not need to be tenderized by long simmering and will have cooked perfectly when brought to a temperature just below boiling point, steaming the molluscs over water (or, better still, wine) vapour is ideal as it lets them release their delicious juices and sea water into the pan to produce a useful stock (albeit sometimes a bit salty) for making a sauce.

Just laying the unopened shells on a hot surface or in the oven will also open them and the insides can then be eaten raw with practically no further preparation.

Oysters and clams can also be eaten raw, provided they are exceptionally fresh and come from recognized beds or facing the open sea. Usually a stubby rigid oyster knife or some similar gadget is necessary to prise them open – competitions are even held to find the person who can open the most in the shortest time!

Crustaceans, which have a shell to protect them instead of a skin, are usually plunged into boiling salted water. For lobster and the like – which are such primitive creatures with undeveloped brains – this is fine. Crab, which are of a higher order, should first be stabbed between the eyes to kill them painlessly and quickly and prevent them from shedding their claws and letting in water. The alternative is to place the lobster or crab in the freezer for 2-3 hours and then deal with them as above or, for lobster, splitting them in half. I have been told that this is

---

ATLANTIC PRAWN – *Usually cooked on the boat and their flavour is excellent. Need shelling. Medium-priced; best buy of the smaller varieties.*

CLAM – *Tiny morsels of meat in comparatively large shells but easily removed from them. Delicious flavour which can become addictive. Can be eaten raw, and so best bought from farms as these are cleaned of mud and other possible toxic impurities.*

CRAB – *Cock crabs have the big claws and hence more of the popular white meat. Hen is cheaper as it has smaller claws. Crabs have very tough shells that must be smashed with a hammer. Medium-priced. Average size is 1.35kg/3lb, producing about 450g/1lb of meat.*

CRAWFISH – *Firmer meat than the lobster and much more of it in relation to the shell, therefore a better buy – if it were not so fished out and increasingly rare.*

*Can be very large (up to 3.2kg/7lb) and these can be tough. No large claws, but makes up for this with its tail meat. Delicious flavour and suitable as alternative to lobster in any dish.*

DUBLIN BAY PRAWN (SCAMPI) – *Looks like a tiny lobster except for the square claws. Buy live and use quickly. Wonderful delicate flavour. Not to be confused with tiger prawns (see opposite). Very expensive, especially large specimens.*

LOBSTER – *Canadian and British varieties are available, but their flavours are very different (British are sweeter; Canadian more pronounced). Convenient size to buy is 675g/1½lb, but make sure they are heavy in relation to their size as they can absorb their own flesh when starved. Expensive. Low ratio of meat to shell. They turn red when cooked.*

now the method recommended by the RSPCA as the most humane means of despatch.

Timing the cooking of a lobster will vary both with species and size. The American ones need a much shorter time as the shell is less dense (10 minutes for a 675g/1½ lb one is usually plenty), but European lobsters take twice as long and large ones progressively longer as the shells become thicker and tougher.

## BUYING AND STORING SHELLFISH

Buy all shellfish from a reputable source, and only accept good heavy ones, as light thin-shelled specimens are a waste of time and money since the flesh has temporarily wasted due to shell-shedding. Of course all fresh crustaceans should be bought live or cooked – simply because otherwise you don't know how long they have been dead. Cook them as soon as you can; if you have to keep them alive, wrap them in seaweed and store in a cool dark place. Kept too long, they absorb their own flesh and deteriorate.

MUSSEL – *Black shiny shells. Must be bought from a source that guarantees they have been purified in clean sea water as they are dirty feeders. Become tough if overcooked. Make good stock. Cheap and good. A large variety (clabby dhhu) is available in Scotland.*

OYSTER – *Pacific variety most readily available all year. Natives generally have better flavour. Mostly eaten raw but can be lightly cooked. The juices are* highly prized. Expensive, but worth it. Buy from reputable dealers for reasons of safety.

SCALLOP – *Excellent source of raw shellfish meat. Easily removed from their shells before cooking. Unfortunately they are traditionally soaked before being sold, but insist on unsoaked ones or you will pay for unwanted water that destroys their texture and flavour. The roe or 'coral' is delicious. Cook just long enough to firm them up or they will* toughen. Expensive, but a little goes a long way. Extra-large ones are fished individually by divers.

SHRIMP – *Small delicious morsels of meat that take a long time to peel in any quantity but are well worth it. Brown Norfolk variety have the best flavour. Medium price because of the bore of shelling. Shelled ones often lack flavour.*

SQUID – *Great disparity in size. Tiny ones cooked and eaten whole. Large ones cleaned and* sliced before cooking. Most delicious when barely cooked. The black ink in their tiny sacs has startling density of colour and is used to delight the eye rather than the palate in risotti and sauces, etc. Medium-priced.

TIGER PRAWN – *Large flat prawn and a useful source of raw shellfish meat as they can be bought frozen. Often used for grilling or barbecuing. Good flavour, which can be quite strong. Tough if overcooked.*

# Lobster Mayonnaise

OPTIONS

*Crawfish, lobster*

3 live lobsters, each weighing
about 675g/1½lb

salt

yolks of 2 hard-boiled eggs,

handful of chopped chives,
to serve (optional)

*for the mayonnaise:*
3 egg yolks

450ml/¾ pint grapeseed oil

1 teaspoon Dijon mustard

few drops of white wine vinegar
or lemon juice

*The type of oil you use for the mayonnaise makes an enormous difference to the flavour. I find olive oil too strong a flavour, so I mix it with a vegetable or groundnut oil. Grapeseed oil gives a very light result, and has the advantage of not becoming too stiff when it is well chilled. Remember, the more oil you feed into the egg yolks the thicker the texture, and any liquid thins it down. The egg yolk acts as the emulsifier.*

*The simpler the dish, the more perfect it has to be. This dish needs an ultra-fresh lobster in peak condition – if you can't be sure it is, do something else with it. I use 3 lobsters for 6 people, as I can dress the tail meat turned over to show its red side on the opposite empty shell. If using larger lobsters, simply divide the meat between the serving plates.*

*As an alternative, you can serve the plain lobster with the Ginger Mayonnaise on page 96.*

First make the mayonnaise: beat the egg yolks with 2 teaspoons of water for 2 minutes. Add the mustard and ½ teaspoon of salt. Blend in the oil, a little at a time, giving the sauce the opportunity to absorb the first lot before adding more. Continue adding the oil until the mixture has reached the chunkiness you desire. Flavour it with a few drops of vinegar or lemon juice. Chill.

Bring a large pan of salted water (285g/10oz salt to 3 litres/5 pints) to the boil. Drop the lobsters into the boiling water and cook for 20 minutes. Lift out and allow to drain. This is the standard procedure for cooking a lobster of this size. Split, clean and use immediately for a plain hot dish; otherwise leave them whole and cool them quickly by holding them briefly under running water, then leave them to cool completely.

When they are quite cold, split the lobsters in half along the back and discard the stomach sac from both sides (you've cut it in half!) and also the intestine which runs down to the vent on the underside from the stomach. Lift out any red coral and crumble it for garnish. Mix some of the greenish pieces (this is the liver, or tomalley) with the mayonnaise for extra flavour, or leave it in. It is a delicacy and not to be discarded.

Remove the tail sections, turn them over red side up and arrange on the opposite tail shell which they will fit into nicely. (A layer of mayonnaise underneath gives a small cushion for them to lie on, and they may be cut into sections for easy eating or decorating).

Crack the claws and remove the meat. Bind it with a little mayonnaise and arrange it in the chest cavity. Decorate with any crumbled coral, or sieved hard-boiled egg yolk mixed with chopped chives if you like.

# Grilled Lobster

3 live lobsters (hens if possible), each weighing about 800g/1¾lb

250g/9oz unsalted butter

1½ tablespoons chopped tarragon

juice of 1 lemon

salt and freshly ground black pepper

*If possible, choose hen lobsters in the hope that they have some coral inside. This looks like a long dark greenish black sac running along the back under the shell. It is pure egg yolk and behaves just like the yolks of ordinary chickens' eggs, though it turns a bright scarlet colour when cooked. When cooked it can be chopped and sprinkled over dishes as a garnish; raw it can be beaten into butter with seasoning and lemon juice and used to baste grilled fish fillets and turn them a beautiful shade of orangey-red. Just as eggs don't taste of chicken, however, nor do lobster eggs taste of lobster, so don't use them for flavouring — just for colouring and thickening.*

Chill the lobsters as per the instructions in the introduction on page 102, then split them in half and remove the stomach and intestine. If you can find it, also remove the little spiky bone attached to the inside of the shell. Break off the big claws. Remove the egg sacs and pound them either with a pestle and mortar, or in the liquidizer with the butter until it is a smooth cream. Add the tarragon, lemon juice to taste and salt and pepper. Preheat the grill to high and place first the claws and then the lobsters, shell side up, underneath it for 2 minutes until they have turned red. Turn them over and spread the flavoured butter generously over the flesh. Turn the claws over as well. Grill the lobsters until the flesh comes away (8-10 minutes), lowering the heat to prevent the meat from drying out.

Lift each lobster half on to a plate and pour over any of the butter that has dripped into the grill pan. Crack the claws and arrange on the plate beside the lobster.

Serve with napkins and finger bowls and accompanied by bowls of rice.

# Fresh Shellfish in Tarragon Butter

*Any shellfish from the order Decapoda of the family Nephropsidae, Palaemonidae, Pandalidae, Crangonidae, Penaeidae and Palinuridae – in other words langoustines or Dublin Bay prawns, lobster, prawns, shrimps and crawfish – are cooked either live or immediately after being killed to avoid loss of juices. Plunging a shrimp into boiling water, I am sure, kills it before any sensation reaches its brain, if it has one. The times of cooking vary not only with size but also with thickness of shell. Undercook rather than overdo.*

Plunge the shellfish into boiling salt (preferably sea) water for 15–20 seconds for the small varieties, up to 20 minutes for a lobster and 25–35 minutes for a large crawfish. If you have underdone it, don't worry because you are going to finish the cooking in the tarragon butter, slicing the larger fish into rounds.

Peel the shrimp family, unless you are seeking some audience participation from your guests.

In a large pan, melt the unsalted butter and throw in the chopped tarragon. Season lightly and bring to the boil.

Add the (shelled) shellfish, stir and add a squeeze of lemon juice if you want a little acidity. (This is not necessary if you are serving a dry white wine with it.)

OPTIONS

*Crawfish, Dublin Bay prawns, lobster, prawns, shrimp*

about 1.25kg/2½lb fresh shellfish (see above)

about 225g/8oz unsalted butter

handful of tarragon, chopped

lemon juice (optional)

salt and freshly ground black pepper

# Moules à la Marinière

3kg/6lb fresh mussels

300ml/½ pint white wine

3 shallots, finely chopped

115g/4oz unsalted butter

1 bay leaf

2 tablespoons chopped parsley

freshly ground black pepper

*If you are out swimming for the day, you will not want to go to the trouble of this recipe to make your mussel soup, as a soup at the seaside just needs cleaned mussels, white wine and butter all steamed together, poured into a large bowl and shared, the mussels probably enjoyed first and the soup slurped down last.*

*However, the sand and beards are always a bit of a nuisance, so I find this is the best way to have the dish at home, taking not much longer but clearing out the nasties.*

Clean the mussels meticulously, pulling out any beards and chipping off anything clinging. Rinse well. Discard any open mussels which do not close when tapped.

Steam the mussels open in the white wine in a tightly covered pan. Turn out into a large colander, letting the juices settle in a bowl placed beneath it.

In a separate pan, fry the shallots in the butter until soft, together with a bay leaf and plenty of ground pepper.

Strain the mussel liquor through a cloth, throw in the chopped parsley and bring everything to the boil.

Divide the mussels between 6 warmed soup plates, discarding any which have not opened, and pour the liquid over.

Serve with a large debris plate for the shells.

# Crab Bisque

*Choose a good heavy hen crab; that way you will avoid paying for the expensive claw meat found in abundance in the big claws of males and only to a lesser extent in the smaller claws of females. It is best used as a garnish as it does not add a great deal of flavour or texture to the soup.*

Clean the crab and chop it up, discarding the stomach and dead men's fingers. Reserve the claw meat for garnish.

Heat the oil in a large pan and fry the carrot, onion, celery, garlic, tomatoes and bouquet garni, stirring from time to time until the mixture browns lightly.

Add the wine mixed with the brandy and reduce until the mixture is dry once again. Add the stocks and the crab chopped up, shell and all. Stir in well. Cover and simmer for 25 minutes.

Stir again and strain, first through a colander to remove the big pieces of shell and then through a sieve, pushing through any vegetables that are soft. Liquidize the soup to make it smooth, adding the rice and tarragon to give texture and flavour and thicken it a little.

Measure the quantity of soup and thin it with either stock or water to make 1 litre/1¾ pints. Add the cream, season (using plenty of pepper) and reheat.

Float any reserved pieces of crab meat in the soup to serve and garnish with the sliced spring onions if you wish.

1 hen crab, weighing about 1.35kg/3lb

3 tablespoons olive oil

2 medium carrots, chopped

2 medium onions, chopped

1 celery stalk, chopped

2 garlic cloves, chopped

4 tomatoes, chopped

bouquet garni

250ml/8fl oz light meat or chicken stock

600ml/1 pint fish stock (page 183), plus more if necessary

2 teaspoons rice, boiled until pulpy

1 tablespoon chopped fresh tarragon

350ml/12fl oz white wine

3 tablespoons brandy

5 tablespoons double cream

salt and freshly ground black pepper

slices of spring onion greens, to garnish (optional)

# Spicy Thai Seafood Soup

OPTIONS
*Prawns, cooked Atlantic prawns,
mussels, scallops, squid rings*

9 raw tiger prawns, peeled,
deveined and halved lengthwise

2kg/4½lb mussels, scrubbed and
debearded, discarding any which do
not close on being tapped

3 large (400ml/14fl oz) tins of
coconut milk

7.5cm/3in piece of fresh ginger,
peeled and sliced

3 red Thai chillies,
deseeded and chopped

6 large stalks of lemon grass,
chopped

1 litre/1¾ pints fish stock
(page 183)

salt and freshly ground black pepper

*for the garnish:*
torn leaves from small bunch
of fresh coriander

3 red Thai chillies, thinly sliced

grated zest of 2 limes

*This soup has an intriguing flavour. The spicy zip of ginger and chillies in no way overwhelms the subtleties of the seafood, lemon grass and coconut. A cross-cultural alternative is to omit the prawns, leave the mussels in their shells and serve the dish in large bowls as a sort of Thai moules à la marinière.*

Pour the coconut milk into a large pan. Add the ginger, chillies, 5 of the lemon grass stalks and the stock. Bring to the boil and simmer gently for 10 minutes to allow the flavours to infuse.

Place the mussels in a separate pan with 125ml/4fl oz water and the remaining lemon grass stalk. Cover tightly, bring to the boil and steam until the mussels open. Remove them as they do so, then carefully remove them from their shells and set aside. Discard any which do not open.

Strain the mussel stock into the coconut broth, taste and adjust the seasoning. Strain the broth, then reheat and add the prawns and mussels and allow to warm through gently for a minute or so.

Serve in warmed wide soup bowls, sprinkle with the coriander leaves, chilli slices and the grated lime zest.

*Variation:* for those allergic to mussels you can make a Thai Scallop Soup, replacing the mussels with 30 queen scallops or normal-size scallops cut into quarters (although the effect is not quite so attractive). Poach the scallops gently in the coconut broth for 30 seconds only until just firm.

# Lobster in Vermouth and Cheese Sauce

OPTIONS
*Any shellfish*

3 freshly boiled 675g/1½lb lobsters
(see page 104)

1 onion, chopped

85g/3oz butter

200ml/7fl oz Noilly Prat white
vermouth

1½ tablespoons flour

600ml/1 pint whipping cream

30g/1oz Gruyère cheese, grated

30g/1oz Parmesan cheese, grated

freshly grated nutmeg to taste

2 teaspoons Dijon mustard

2 tablespoons toasted and sieved
breadcrumbs

salt and freshly ground black pepper

*This is the dish we used in the restaurant when anyone asked for lobster thermidor – which, although classic, is not in my repertoire. This has many similar ingredients, but it isn't quite so 'mustardy' and I prefer it. You can assemble it in advance, but then it has to be reheated slowly in the oven and finished off by browning under the grill, so I usually both assemble and finish it quickly at the last minute.*

Cook the lobsters and cool as described on pages 104-5. This can be done in advance.

In a heavy-based pan, cook the onion in the butter until soft but not brown. Add the vermouth and boil until it has all but disappeared. Stir in the flour, mix well and add the cream. Bring to the boil and simmer for 5 minutes, stirring frequently. Add the cheeses, nutmeg to taste and the mustard. Season and cover with film or a lid to trap the steam in and prevent a skin from forming.

Carefully slit the lobsters lengthwise in half to use the shell for serving and discard the stomach and intestine (see pages 104-5). Crack the claws, remove the meat and also that from the body. Cut it all into bite-sized pieces. Place in a bowl and cover with film to keep it moist.

About 10 minutes before serving, preheat a very hot grill. Reheat the sauce to just below boiling and mix in the lobster to warm through gently, but do not allow it to boil or the lobster will release its juices and the sauce will thin out.

Divide the sauce and lobster between the shells, sprinkle with crumbs and place under the hot grill to brown.

# Prawns in Cumin and Coconut Sauce

*This quick and easy dish makes a very mild fish curry. I usually serve it along with other curries as part of an Indian-style meal, with basmati rice and some hot chutneys for those who like their food spicier.*

In a frying pan, cook the onion in the oil with 2 tablespoons of water until the onion is soft.

Add the ginger and then the ground cumin. Fry them gently together until aromatic. Add the fish stock and creamed coconut. Simmer until the mixture forms a thin paste.

Add the prawns and cook gently until they are firm and cooked. Season.

Garnish with a few whole coriander or parsley leaves to serve.

OPTIONS

*Any crustacean*

30 raw medium-sized tiger prawns, shelled and deveined

1 onion

2 tablespoons grapeseed or groundnut oil

1 teaspoon peeled and grated root ginger

2 tablespoons ground cumin

150ml/¼ pint fish stock (page 183)

½ block (100g/3½oz) of creamed coconut

few coriander or flat-leaved parsley leaves, to garnish

# Mixed Shellfish in Baked Tomatoes

OPTIONS
*Clams, mussels, squid*

2kg/4½lb mixed shellfish

115g/4oz fresh breadcrumbs

5 tablespoons olive oil

5 large beef tomatoes, halved

2 shallots, finely chopped

3 spring onions,
sliced on the diagonal

2 garlic cloves, crushed

150ml/¼ pint white wine

1 tablespoon mixed chopped fresh
thyme, parsley and marjoram or basil

150ml/¼ pint fish stock (page 183)

salt and freshly ground black pepper

*This makes a good light Italian-style lunch dish, which is especially good if you use fresh marjoram. An ideal mix of shellfish for this dish would be about 1.1 litres/2 pints each of mussels and clams with 450g/1lb of squid. The stuffing can be made in advance and kept in the refrigerator, but don't fill the tomatoes until you are ready to cook them or they will go soggy.*

Prepare and steam any clams and mussels, then remove them from their shells as described on pages 116 and 108 respectively. Prepare and cook any squid as described on page 136 (without the other flavouring ingredients).

Preheat the oven to 220°C/425°F/gas7.

Fry the breadcrumbs in the oil until lightly toasted, then remove from the pan with a slotted spoon and drain.

Halve 3 of the tomatoes and hollow out the tomato halves. Season the insides, turn them upside down and leave to drain. Skin, halve and deseed the remaining tomatoes.

Sauté the shallots and spring onions in the oil that remains in the pan until they start to soften. Add the garlic, chopped tomatoes, wine and herbs and simmer until dry. Add the stock and reduce by half.

Mix in the prepared shellfish and bind with the fried crumbs. Pile this mixture into the tomato cases and bake in the hot oven until the outside has softened but not collapsed, about 15 minutes.

Finish under a preheated hot grill to brown the top lightly.

# Crab Soufflés

*Make this soufflé in advance and only cook it just before you want to serve it. It is not a true soufflé, as the egg whites are not beaten separately and then folded into the mixture, but it rises just as well. Have your guests ready at the table so that they can eat the dish as soon as it comes from the oven.*

Preheat the oven to 250°C/475°F/gas9 and grease 6 ramekins with 15g/½oz of the butter.

Pick over the crab carefully to get rid of any pieces of residual shell mixed in it. Turn the meat into a liquidizer with the eggs and extra yolks.

Melt the remaining butter in a heavy-based saucepan, stir in the flour and cook this roux for a minute or so, stirring. Add the milk and stir vigorously. Allow to cool a little and then pour into the blender or food processor and blend everything together. Add the anchovy essence and adjust the seasoning.

Pour the mixture into each of the buttered ramekins to fill them to two-thirds of the way up. Place them in a bain-marie, or baking tin lined with wet newspaper and half-filled with hot water, and cook in the oven for 8 minutes, or until the soufflés are well risen. (If you have made the mixture in advance to this point and chilled it, it will take 20 minutes to heat up and soufflé).

Serve immediately with hollandaise sauce. It will not wait.

1 medium-sized cooked hen crab

40g/1½oz butter

2 whole eggs, plus 2 extra egg yolks

30g/1oz flour

300ml/½ pint milk

1 teaspoon anchovy essence

Hollandaise Sauce (page 184) flavoured with lemon juice to taste, to serve

salt and freshly ground black pepper

# Clams and Pasta Shells

OPTIONS

*Clams, mussels, smoked fish*

2.75kg/6lb clams

450ml/¾ pint dry white wine

450g/1lb pasta shells

4 tablespoons olive oil

1 red onion, finely chopped

2 garlic cloves, finely chopped

6 spring onions, finely sliced on the diagonal

150ml/¼ pint double cream

150ml/¼ pint whipping cream

salt and freshly ground black pepper

freshly grated Parmesan cheese, to serve (optional)

*You are more likely to find fresh clams in small fish shops near the local fish markets, otherwise they can be bought by mail order and delivered direct (see page 192), so there is no reason why they should not be more widely used.*

*You will probably find a lot of sand inside the shells of the clams, which will be released only when they open in the heat of the steam. With the sand, however, come the juices; so just add more water, stir well and let it settle. Then strain through a 'J' cloth and boil to reduce it to full strength again.*

In a large heavy-based saucepan which has a tight-fitting lid, bring the wine to the boil and add all the clams. Cover with the lid and cook over a high heat until it comes to the boil again. Open and stir the shells around to redistribute them. Replace the lid and repeat the operation.

Place a large sieve over a bowl or pan, tip the clams into this and pour half a kettleful of hot water over them to release the grit and juices, reserve the liquid in the bowl or pan.

Rinse the pan in which you have cooked the clams, fill with fresh water, add salt and put over a high heat. Pick the clams out of their shells and set aside. Discard the shells.

Cook the pasta in the pan of boiling salted water until just al dente. Drain and moisten with half the oil. Keep warm.

In a large heavy-based pan, fry together the chopped red onion and the garlic in the remaining oil until slightly softened, carefully strain in the clam water through a cloth and boil it down vigorously to 150ml/¼ pint.

Add the sliced green part of the spring onions and the creams, adjust the seasoning and bring to the boil for 30 seconds. Reheat the pasta in this and fold in the clams. Pepper well.

Serve in warmed shallow bowls, with grated Parmesan if you like it (I do, but it's not strictly correct with this type of dish).

# Mixed Shellfish in a Cream and Curry Sauce

*The spicy sea smell of fresh shellfish goes well with a light dusting of curry powder softened with cream. Serve this dish on a bed of cooked shredded lettuce, pepped up with a little sorrel or watercress.*

*If you are using lobster or crawfish, they must be cooked in advance, shelled and sliced into bite-sized pieces before use.*

Shred the lettuce and the other greens and cook in the butter in a frying pan for 2-3 minutes until they have softened and wilted. Season and add the curry powder, lemon juice and two-thirds of the cream. Simmer for 2 minutes. Strain, reserving the sauce and keeping the greens warm.

Steam the shellfish lightly according to type over a very little water, discard the shells or remove them. Strain the resulting juices from the cooking into the sauce.

Add the coriander if using and reduce by boiling away to 300ml/½ pint. Take off the heat. Mix the egg yolks with the rest of the cream and stir this into the sauce.

Add the shellfish and reheat, but being careful not to allow it to boil or liquid will come out of the shellfish and the egg will overcook. Adjust the seasoning, if necessary.

Divide the wilted greens between 6 plates, pile the shellfish on top and pour on the sauce.

OPTIONS
*Clams, crawfish, lobster, mussels, oysters, tiger prawns*

1.25kg/2½ lb mixed shellfish

2 little gem lettuces

5 large sorrel leaves or 1 bunch of watercress, stalks removed

50g/2oz butter

1 teaspoon curry powder

juice of ½ lemon

175ml/6fl oz whipping cream

2 teaspoons chopped coriander (optional)

2 egg yolks

salt and freshly ground black pepper

# Scallops in Lemon, Ginger and Vermouth Sauce

*Your scallops must be unsoaked (see page 103) or they won't brown delicately. Ask your fishmonger and don't let him put you off, but do give him time to obtain what you want.*

First make the sauce (and get plates hot ready for serving): melt the butter in a heavy frying pan and add the Noilly Prat, ginger and lemon zest. Boil to reduce to about 1 tablespoon of liquid. Taste, and if you want a strong ginger flavour, add 150ml/¼ pint water and continue boiling until the flavour is strong enough. Add the fish stock and boil down to 150ml/¼ pint.

Now add the cream. Strain into a clean pan, reduce to 350ml/12fl oz and season. Divide the sauce between the warmed serving plates and keep warm.

Rinse out the original pan, lightly brush it with oil and heat until very hot (you can achieve a higher temperature with oil before it burns than with butter).

Season the scallops and prick any corals a couple of times to prevent them from bursting when they cook. Then brown the scallops VERY quickly in the red-hot pan for about 20 seconds on each side. Cook them in a couple of batches so that you only have one layer lying in the pan, keeping the heat high. Do the same with any corals.

Pile 5 on each plate, garnish with a little of the cooked ginger slices cut into strips, the lemon zest and any corals.

15 scallops, halved into 2 thin discs, or 30 small ones

30g/1oz butter

2 tablespoons Noilly Prat white vermouth

5cm/2in piece of root ginger, peeled and sliced

grated or pared zest of 1 uncoated lemon

150ml/¼ pint fish stock (page 183)

300ml/½ pint whipping cream

2 tablespoons grapeseed or groundnut oil

salt and freshly ground black pepper

# Prawns in Jackets

OPTIONS
*Cooked prawns, mussels,
shrimp, squid in rings*

60 cooked Atlantic prawns, shelled

3 large baking potatoes

2 tablespoons grapeseed or
groundnut oil

115g/4oz butter

50g/2oz flour

350ml/12fl oz milk

115g/4oz Cheddar cheese

salt and freshly ground black pepper

chopped chives,
to garnish (optional)

*This recipe can be adapted for any fish. For special occasions use
the white wine sauce on page 120 to mix with the potato and
stick some prawn heads in around the edge for garnish.*

Preheat the oven to 200°C/400°F/gas6.

Rub the skins of the potatoes with oil and salt and bake for
about 45-60 minutes until soft.

When the potatoes are cool enough to handle, cut them in half
and scoop out the middle, leaving enough sides to keep the potato
shells firm. Mash the scooped-out potato flesh with half the butter
and some seasoning.

Melt the remaining butter in a heavy-based saucepan, stir in
the flour and cook this roux for a minute or so, stirring. Add the
milk and stir vigorously to make a thick and smooth white sauce.
Stir in half the cheese and season to taste.

Preheat a hot grill. Bind the potato with as much sauce as
necessary to give a moist consistency, reserving about 6
tablespoons. Stir in the prawns, reserving a few for garnish if you
like, and refill the skins. Top with the reserved sauce, sprinkle with
the remaining cheese and brown under the grill.

Serve garnished with a few reserved prawns and chopped
chives if you like.

# Scallops with Pernod and Cream

*What do tarragon, star anise and Pernod have in common? An aniseed-like flavour, which goes with chicken nearly as well as with fish. Mushroom soaks up the flavour too, but lengthy cooking destroys it.*

Slice each of the scallops into 2 thin discs, trimming off any corals, and set both aside.

In a frying pan, soften the spring onions and garlic in 50g/2oz of the butter for 5 minutes, add the mushrooms and cook for a further 5 minutes. Add the fish stock and bring to the boil. Simmer the scallops and coral in this mixture for just long enough to firm them up, about 2 minutes. Remove with a slotted spoon and keep warm.

Strain the liquid into another pan, reserving the solids. Boil to reduce it by half and add the creams. Bring to the boil and reduce to a coating consistency. Add in the Pernod, simmer gently and finish by whisking in a little butter.

Season to taste, fold in the mushrooms, etc. and the scallops with their juices. Divide between 6 warmed plates and sprinkle with a little chopped tarragon to serve.

15 scallops

½ bunch of spring onions, sliced on the diagonal

½ garlic clove

85g/3oz butter

225g/8oz button mushrooms

150ml/¼ pint double cream

150ml/¼ pint whipping cream

150ml/¼ pint Pernod

300ml/½ pint fish stock (page 183)

salt and freshly ground black pepper

chopped tarragon, to serve

# Potted Prawns

OPTIONS

*Atlantic prawns, crab meat, shrimp*

1.35kg/3lb raw Atlantic prawns in the shell (to produce 225g/8oz shelled)

115g/4oz slightly salted butter

blade of mace

freshly grated nutmeg to taste

cayenne pepper to taste

1 tablespoon medium sweet sherry

toasted brown bread, to serve

*There are very few times when I use raw alcohol in a dish. Brandy butter is one and this is another.*

*To clarify butter, melt it over a gentle heat until it separates, then allow it to rest. Skim away any scum, and then pour off the clear liquid sitting on top (this is the clarified butter), leaving behind the solids on the bottom.*

*Poured over the pots of prawns, it makes an airtight seal and the sherry helps to preserve them as well – even so, don't keep them for more than a week.*

Peel the prawns. Put the prawns in one heavy-based pan and put the shells in another large heavy-based pan with half the butter and the mace. Over a gentle heat, slowly melt this butter until hot, stirring from time to time. Do not bring to the boil, just get it very hot, otherwise it will turn oily and separate. Now strain the butter over the prawns.

Add the spices and sherry, and reheat stirring occasionally as before. Allow to cool, give a final mix and adjust the seasoning, if necessary. Turn the prawns into, traditionally, little pots or ramekins.

Melt and clarify the remaining butter and pour over the tops of the pots of prawns to make a seal about 5mm/¼in deep. Chill in the refrigerator until set.

Remove from the refrigerator and allow to come to room temperature before serving with the toast.

# Scallops with Bacon and Noisette Butter

*Scallops are a gift to any cook, so long as you can cook them at the last minute. Overcook them and they turn into tough bullets. They adapt themselves to any type of recipe – fried, creamy, spiced or cold – and even their trimmings make good stock. The muscle is pure protein and makes the smoothest of quenelles. This dish is an adaptation of the traditional way of serving skate with black butter.*

*A good way of getting bacon really crisp is to finish it briefly in the microwave cooker on high.*

15 scallops

225g/8oz thinly sliced streaky bacon, cut into batons

175g/6oz butter

125ml/4fl oz raspberry vinegar

salt and freshly ground black pepper

Heat a large frying pan and lay the bacon in one layer on the base with half the butter. Cook vigorously to release the fat. Using a slotted spoon if possible, remove the bacon when it is really crisp. Crumble into small pieces.

Increase the heat to high to get the pan really hot. Sear the scallops for 20 seconds on each side in the very hot pan (in two batches if necessary) and transfer them to warmed serving plates. Sprinkle them with the bacon.

Reheat the pan over a gentle heat, add the rest of the butter and cook it to a tawny brown. Add the raspberry vinegar and reduce this to a syrup. Season and pour over the scallops.

# Crab Wonton Parcels

*These make delicious hot large mouthfuls, but they must be well seasoned. You will need to make at least 4 (preferably 5) turns in the pastry to enclose the crab mixture properly. The parcels will have to be cooked in batches, so be sure you have the oil at a good temperature at the beginning of each batch.*

In a heavy-based pan, heat the oil and cook the onion, chilli and ginger until soft. Add the crab meat, creamed coconut, spring onions, cornflour slaked in a spoonful of water and the cream. Simmer until thick and bound together. Adjust the seasoning with salt, pepper and a drop or two of soy sauce.

Cut the wonton wrappers in three lengthwise into wide strips. Starting at one end of each, place 1 large teaspoon of the mixture centred just in from that long end. Fold that end diagonally over the mixture to enclose it and then fold the triangle that has formed over again. Keep on folding this way until it forms a compact parcel. Seal the end of the triangle with a very little water. Repeat until all the wrappers and mixture have been used. Let the stuffed wontons rest in the fridge to set, about 30 minutes.

Deep-fry the wontons in batches in hot oil until crisp, draining on paper towels and keeping each batch warm until all are cooked. Serve as soon as they are, garnished with some curls of spring onion if you wish and with soy sauce for dipping.

350g/12oz fresh crab meat

2 tablespoons grapeseed or groundnut oil

1 medium onion, finely chopped

3 small green chillies, deseeded and sliced

$1\frac{1}{2}$ tablespoons peeled and grated root ginger

2 tablespoon creamed coconut (optional)

4-5 spring onions, thinly sliced on the diagonal

2 teaspoons cornflour

5 tablespoons double cream

few drops of good-quality soy sauce, plus more for dipping

16 wonton wrappers (23x23cm/9x9in)

salt and freshly ground black pepper

grapeseed or groundnut oil, for deep-frying

more spring onions, to garnish (optional)

# Lobster Salad

1 lobster, weighing about 675g/1½lb, cooked, shelled and cut into pieces

50g/2oz mixed salad leaves

chopped chives, to garnish

*for the vinaigrette:*
175ml/6fl oz olive oil

1 teaspoon soy sauce

1 teaspoon Dijon mustard

juice of 1 lemon

pinch of sugar

2 teaspoons Pernod

1 teaspoon each of chopped tarragon, parsley and chives

salt and freshly ground black pepper

*Lobster salad is one of the best ways of using up leftover cooked lobster meat, or just a great treat at any time. Go for a colourful mix of salad leaves and try to include a good balance of flavours; with some sharp-tasting leaves, such as curly endive, a few sweet leaves like lamb's lettuce or torn butterhead lettuce, and a bit of punch from something like rocket.*

Mix all the vinaigrette ingredients together well with seasoning to taste, shaking or whisking to emulsify it.

Toss the lobster pieces in the vinaigrette and leave to marinate in the refrigerator for about 30 minutes.

Arrange some of the salad on each of 6 plates. Arrange the lobster on top. Sprinkle with any lobster coral, crumbled, and the remaining vinaigrette. Garnish with chopped chives to serve.

*Serves 2*

# Crab Potato Fritters

225g/8oz cooked potato

2 tablespoons plain flour

3 small (size-4) eggs

2 tablespoons milk

meat from 1 medium cooked crab

1 tablespoon chopped parsley

grapeseed or groundnut oil, for frying

salt and freshly ground black pepper

*These pancakes/fritters can be served instead of potatoes as an accompaniment to poached or steamed cutlets, or a large thick one can serve as a picnic slice or a base for grilled cheese.*

In a food processor, blend the potatoes with the flour, then the eggs and finally the milk.

Turn the mixture into a bowl and add the crab meat and chopped parsley. Season.

Heat the oil in a frying pan and drop several large spoonfuls of the mixture into it. Cook fairly briskly, until the edges begin to brown, then turn the fritters over and fry the other sides.

Serve as soon as possible.

*Variation:* Make smoked haddock cakes in exactly the same way, substituting 115g/4oz of flaked, smoked haddock for the crab meat and cooking the mixture in slightly larger spoonfuls. Season generously with pepper but be careful with the salt as the fish is probably already quite salty. You could also replace the chopped parsley with chives. Serve for breakfast with grilled bacon.

# Mediterranean Fish Salad

*Any cooked seafood will work well with this treatment, but the selection used here will give a more successful Mediterranean type of mix. Be generous with the basil and try to get some of the vine-ripened plum tomatoes now more widely available in our supermarkets for real flavour.*

In a large sauté or frying pan, sauté the shallots in the oil until soft. Add the tomatoes and white wine. Boil to reduce until it begins to fry. Add the stock, basil and seasoning. Reduce again until the oil begins to show again. Adjust the seasoning.

Throw in the squid and scallops, stir and allow to stiffen a little. Remove from the heat and add the other shellfish. Adjust the seasoning if necessary, allow to cool and then chill.

OPTIONS
*Clams, cooked shelled lobster, mussels, prawns, scallops, squid*

3 small squid, cleaned and sliced

4 scallops, each cut into 2 thin discs

24 clams, steamed open
(see page 116)

15 mussels, steamed open
(see page 108)

5 shallots, chopped

125ml/4fl oz olive oil

4 tomatoes, skinned,
deseeded and finely diced

125ml/4fl oz white wine

150 ml/¼ pint fish stock (page 183)

small handful of basil, torn

salt and freshly ground black pepper

# Bavarois of Prawns and Egg

*This makes a cold lunch dish or can form part of a buffet. When mixing two ingredients like jellied fish stock and cream, try to make both the same density, as this results in them mixing more easily. If the stock has not jellied enough, the cream floats to the top and won't mix. (If you are short of stock, use tinned consommé instead, with a little bit of extra gelatine).*

Hard-boil the eggs. Shell them, separate the yolks from the whites and chop the whites evenly. Dissolve the gelatine in the fish stock.

Make a paste of the egg yolks with some of the fish stock and mix in the anchovy essence. Thin the paste out so that there are no lumps, gradually adding the rest of the stock. Set aside to cool and to start to gel a little.

When the stock has the texture of raw egg whites, whip the cream until it is just firm and no longer runny. Fold it into the stock and add the chopped whites and shrimps. Season carefully.

Turn the mixture into a bowl (or into a mould if you wish to turn it out to present it) and chill thoroughly overnight.

Unmould by dipping briefly in hot water and then turning out or serve from the bowl. Garnish with whole prawns and the chervil or parsley.

OPTIONS
*Any shelled crustacean*

6 eggs

300ml/½ pint well-flavoured fish stock (page 183)

9 gelatine leaves or crystals for 850ml/1½ pints of liquid

2 teaspoons anchovy essence

300ml/½ pint whipping cream

450g/1lb cooked prawns, shelled

salt and freshly ground black pepper

*for the garnish:*
12 whole cooked prawns

chervil or parsley sprigs

# Mussel and Couscous Salad

OPTIONS

*Clams, mussels, prawns, shrimp*

3.5 litres/6 pints mussels

150 ml/¼ pint dry white wine

285g/10 oz quick-cook couscous

175ml/6fl oz olive oil

450g/1lb tomatoes, skinned, deseeded and diced

3 basil leaves, torn into shreds

85g/3oz watercress, cut into strips, plus more to garnish

salt and freshly ground black pepper

*Lots of mussels on their own can be quite strong. I often feel they need a 'diluting' medium, like rice or couscous, to spread their flavour. Their stock is invaluable, but always keep it separate from your usual fish stock as many people are severely allergic to mussels. You can also serve this dish warm.*

Cook the mussels in the wine as described on page 108. Strain the juices through a cloth and set the mussels aside.

Mix the juices with water to make up to 450ml/¾ pint and simmer the couscous in it according to packet instructions. Drain if necessary. Stir in the oil and leave to cool.

Fold the tomato dice, watercress and basil strips into the couscous with the mussels. Season and chill.

Serve garnished with more sprigs of watercress.

# Squid in Batter

*As with most shellfish, squid vary enormously in size. So, unless you have very small ones which are ideal for frying, they must be prepared as on page 189. Cooking them in hot oil means that they are ready in seconds. As soon as the outsides are brown and crisp, the insides are ready too. Don't add the egg whites to the batter until you are ready to fry.*

Pour the cider or beer into a jug. In a large bowl, mix together the flour and the tablespoon of oil and add the cider, slowly to prevent any lumps forming. Add the rosemary and salt.

Whisk the egg white in another bowl until it stands in soft peaks. Fold it into the flour-and-cider mixture.

Heat the oil for deep-frying until it toasts a piece of dry bread quickly in 20 seconds. Put all the squid into the batter, then lift the pieces out one at a time and carefully place them in the hot oil (not dropping them from a great height or you will get burnt). As soon as the pieces brown, lift them out and drain on paper towels.

Serve them either with the cold tomato sauce or just a squeeze of lemon.

675g/1½lb squid,
cut into strips, rings or pieces

150ml/½ pint dry cider
or light beer

4 tablespoons flour

1 tablespoon grapeseed
or groundnut oil

1 teaspoon ground dried rosemary
(optional)

white of 1 egg

1 teaspoon salt

grapeseed or groundnut oil,
for deep-frying

cold Tomato Sauce (page 186),
to serve (optional)

lemon wedges,
to serve (optional)

# Shellfish Brochettes with Chilli Dipping Sauce

*This is a recipe with lots of possibilities. Brochettes immediately suggest a wonderful hands-on sort of dish, where finger bowls or hot towels will be absolutely necessary. Because your guests will already be getting their fingers dirty, you can leave the shells on the prawns and cook them that way – the result is an incredible spicy flavour. If you think that's too unsophisticated for your guests, shell the prawns but leave their little tail fins on; then you keep some of that spicy flavour, but eliminate a lot of the mess.*

*Yet another possibility is to eliminate the skewers. Just pan-fry the dish on top of the stove. You can peel the prawns but fry the shells with the prawns and discard them before serving to give all of the flavour but none of the mess.*

225g/8oz queen scallops or unsoaked large scallops

450g/1lb raw king prawns

grapeseed or groundnut oil, for the skewers

lime wedges, to serve (optional)

*for the marinade:*
3 tablespoons soy sauce

1 tablespoon runny honey

2 garlic cloves, crushed

4 tablespoons grapeseed or groundnut oil

2 chillies

2 spring onions

Leave queen scallops whole. Cut larger scallops in quarters, removing and trimming any orange coral. Leave prawns in their shells or remove all but the tail fins as above.

Blend the marinade ingredients together in a liquidizer, pour it into a shallow dish and toss the scallops and prawns in it. Leave them to marinate for half an hour, turning them occasionally.

Oil 6 skewers (soak them first if they are wooden) and thread the scallops and prawns on them, placing the orange corals at strategic intervals. Grill the skewers for 5 minutes or less, turning them as needed.

Boil up the remaining marinade briefly in a small pan to make the dipping sauce.

Serve with the dipping sauce and lime wedges if you wish. These brochettes are wonderful on a bed of boiled or steamed rice spiced up with finely sliced chillies, spring onions and chopped hard-boiled egg.

# Squid in Garlic, Mushrooms and Lemon Juice

1.25kg/2½lb medium-sized squid (with or without tentacles), cleaned and cut into rings

3 slices of bread, crusts removed and each cut into 4 triangles

175ml/6fl oz olive oil

1 bunch of celery leaves or parsley

2 garlic cloves

115g/4oz button mushrooms, sliced

lemon juice to taste

salt and freshly ground black pepper

*Unless squid are very big, their flesh needs only just enough cooking to heat it through, as the more it cooks the tougher it becomes until it needs to be stewed thoroughly for hours like shin of beef to get it tender again. Like all small pieces of fish, a last-minute application of heat is all that is needed. Care has to go into what goes with it and this need not be complicated to be delicious.*

In a large frying pan, fry the triangles of bread in all but 2 tablespoons of the oil until crisp. Remove from the pan and drain on paper towels. Throw the celery or parsley leaves into the pan and fry them until crisp (keeping your face well out of spitting range!) Lift out and drain on paper towels. Pour off any oil left in the pan (reserve for another occasion).

Mix the rest of the fresh oil with the garlic and heat it until the garlic begins to brown. Add the sliced mushrooms and cook gently until soft, then add the lemon juice mixed with 2 tablespoons of water. Turn up the heat and add the squid. Season and cook until they are just hot through, they should have turned opaque and the liquid will not be too plentiful.

Serve on the fried bread triangles, with the fried celery leaves sprinkled over.

# Angels on Horseback

*This is turning the clock back and giving a savoury recipe for a starter. However, oysters are becoming very popular again and this recipe is especially good for those who cannot bear to eat them raw. Traditionally these are served on crisp oblongs of bread fried in butter.*

Preheat the grill to moderate to high. Roll half a thin rasher of the bacon around each of the oysters and impale 6 of the wrapped oysters on each of 6 skewers.

Brush with a little hot oil and grill them, turning from time to time to cook the bacon, but keeping the cooking time to a minimum, about 5 minutes.

Season with pepper to serve.

*Variation:* For scallops on horseback, give scallops (12 fat ones, each sliced into 3 discs) exactly the same treatment, but use ribbons of smoked salmon (about 115g/4oz) instead of the bacon and skewer any pieces of scallop coral in between to give an extra splash of colour. Cook for a few minutes only, until the scallops are just firm. Serve on a bed of mixed green leaves.

OPTIONS
*Oysters, fresh smoked oysters*

36 shelled oysters

18 rashers of streaky bacon

grapeseed or groundnut oil, heated

freshly ground black pepper

# mixed catch

*All over the world local cuisines feature dishes of mixed fish and shellfish, especially the sea stews for which the Mediterranean is famous, not to mention the spicier offerings from further East*

This section is our catch-all to include recipes for things like smoked fish, fish roes as well as recipes where more than one type of fish is used – they may be round, flat or shellfish (or all three), like the alliance of sole, scallops and crawfish on page 164. This is a classic partnership, well known to blend together amazingly with a very satisfying texture and flavour. Technically you can change the blend, though I have never found a combination that satisfies quite so well.

Obviously in cases of mixed fish, the individual cooking times will vary according to shape and density. The fish that require the longest cooking (i.e. dense-fleshed fish like tuna or oily fish like mackerel) must therefore be started first and the shorter-cooking varieties (like the white fish) added later so that they all finish together. Lobsters and other crustaceans included here are usually boiled in advance as they have to be shelled before being used and are generally added at the last minute just to warm them through.

Several recipes in this section are for specific fish and for which there are no options, like that for smoked mackerel or for the soft herring roe (though I imagine that other types of soft roe are suitable for such simple treatment).

## SMOKING FISH

This might be a good place to explain smoking. Fish for smoking is first subjected to a curing process, usually salting, and then goes on to being enveloped by delicious wood-smelling smoke.

There are two types of smoking used for fish: cold-smoking and hot-smoking. In the first, lengthier process, the food is kept at some distance from the heat source, so the smoke has cooled considerably by the time it reaches the fish. Fish smoked this way keep better and generally require further cooking (usually by poaching), as with kippered herrings or smoked haddock, and are served hot. In the case of salmon, cod's roe and halibut, on the other hand, the resulting food is generally sliced very thinly and eaten raw and cold.

In hot-smoking the raw fish is much closer to

SMOKED COD – *smoked cod fillets are now very difficult to find as they are almost always dyed.*

SMOKED HADDOCK – *Undyed fillets now more common but more expensive. Good flavour and moist texture. 'Finnan haddies' are whole small haddock cold-smoked.*

SMOKED HALIBUT – *Thinly sliced, it can be eaten raw like smoked salmon. Moist and full of flavour but expensive.*

SMOKED HERRING – *Commonly called kipper. Still good value, although undyed more expensive. Dyed fish are generally deep brown in colour.*

SMOKED MACKEREL – *Oily fish often sold in hot-smoked fillets and sometimes peppered. Very good value and versatile.*

SMOKED TROUT – *Hot-smoked fillets and whole rainbow trout available. Some dyed (darker in colour). Needs no further cooking.*

SMOKED SALMON – *Best is Scottish fish smoked in Scotland, but beware as much inferior Pacific salmon now smoked in Scotland. Look for good pink (not orange) colour. Expensive, but trimmings excellent value for pâtés. mousses, etc.*

SMOKED SALMON TROUT – *Prepared as smoked salmon and just as expensive. Flavour preferred by many.*

SALT COD – *Mediterranean favourite anomalously mostly produced in Scandinavia.*

*Spanish variety most readily obtainable in this country. Expensive. Need lengthy soaking before use.*

COD'S ROE – *Usually sold salted and ready-poached. Can be eaten as they are but are more usually sliced and fried. Very good value. Often smoked.*

SOFT HERRING ROES – *Also known as milt, this is the sperm of the male fish and is regarded as a great delicacy.*

the heat and therefore smoked for a shorter time. The results, as in the case of smoked mackerel, are almost entirely cooked; but it produces a moist-but-dry effect – you can tell the fish has never seen steam – and the results may be eaten as they are or simply warmed through. Sometimes it is fun to use such fish hot, as in the pasta dish on page 158.

Unfortunately a great deal of smoked fish on sale nowadays – especially smoked white fish like cod and haddock – has been dyed to give it the colour of properly smoked fish without the benefit of the full (time-consuming and therefore expensive) treatment. Truly smoked fish is usually much paler and less exotically coloured. Try to specify undyed fish to your fishmonger, as they have much more flavour and are well worth the extra cost. With herrings and some other fish, a good indication of the genuine article is a hole pierced through the head to allow the fishes to be threaded and hung up in the smokehouse.

# Lady Curzon's Fish Soup

1 onion, chopped

30g/1oz butter

2 or 3 teaspoons curry paste

850ml/1½ pints well-flavoured
fish stock (page 183)

½ tablespoon flour

400ml/14fl oz coconut milk

300ml/½ pint whipping cream,
whipped to soft peaks

salt and freshly ground black pepper

*I've cheated by using Lady Curzon's name; her own soup is curried chicken topped with cold whipped cream and browned under the grill. This version has a curried fish soup underneath. It looks stunning and not many realize that whipped cream browns under the grill.*

In a large heavy-based pan, sweat the onions in the butter until they are soft, adding water if necessary to achieve this.

Add the curry paste and the flour and fry for 3 minutes. Then add the stock and simmer, stirring from time to time, until smooth and thickened. Simmer until the flavour has matured, about half an hour.

Preheat a hot grill. Add the coconut milk to the soup, adjust the seasoning and strain, if you prefer the onion removed.

Arrange 6 deep heatproof bowls on a baking sheet or tray which will fit under the grill and pour the soup into them to just below the top. Float the cream on top of the soup and brown under the grill.

# Cornish Fish Chowder

*This is called a Cornish chowder, or stew-cum-soup, because it is made with all the natural flavourings we have down here. The hedges have plenty of garlic and sorrel to give acidity and pungency, and the local salt pork is mild but with enough fat to oil the fish and give body to the soup. For the fish... well the choice is huge. Since the dish is really for home cooking, there's no point in specifying expensive fish, but if a lobster happened to drop in it wouldn't come amiss, nor would a bass or turbot.*

*The Cornish 'chibble' or 'chibol' for spring onion comes from the French chiboule.*

OPTIONS

*Cod, coley, haddock, halibut, monkfish, pollack, rock salmon, swordfish, squid*

1 cod's head, 3 skate 'nobs' (or 115g/4oz cod fillets), 1 small red mullet, scaled and cut across into 6, 1 small grey mullet, scaled and cut across into 6, 1 small skate wing, skinned and filleted, 18 whole prawns, 18 queen scallops

85g/3oz salt pork cut in chunks, rind removed

50g/2oz pork dripping (or similar)

2 onions, coarsely chopped

675g/1½lb peeled potato, cut into chunks

1 teaspoon dried thyme

2 bay leaves

3 garlic cloves, chopped

6 juniper berries

1 teaspoon crushed black peppercorns

6 spring onions

about 20 sorrel leaves

1 tablespoon balsamic vinegar or Worcestershire sauce

salt and freshly ground black pepper

In a frying pan, simmer the salt pork in the dripping or other fat and 150ml/¼ pint of water for about 20 minutes to soften it. Then turn up the heat to evaporate the water and continue to cook the pork until it begins to fry in the fat.

Add the onions, potatoes, thyme, bay leaves, garlic, juniper berries and peppercorns. Stir until the mixture begins to brown. Add the cod's head and whole spring onions. Pour in water to cover and bring to the boil. Simmer gently for about 20 minutes until the potato is soft. Discard the cod's head, except for the cheek muscles to put back in later. Check the seasoning to see how much more salt is needed (remember the salt pork), having also checked the quantity of liquid. There should be enough to cook the pieces of fish without it being watery.

Add the sorrel leaves and chunks of white fish, bring it all back to the boil and simmer for a further 5 minutes.

Add the prawns, scallops, cod's cheek and skate wing and cook for about 5 minutes to cook and firm them up. If you find the soup a little bland add a shake or two of balsamic vinegar or Worcestershire sauce.

# *Fish Broth with Pesto*

*This russet-coloured soup looks beautiful with a splendid dollop of pesto spooned into the centre (another terrific excuse for eating pesto). This is a soup for high summer, when the basil has big leaves and a strong peppery flavour.*

*Try to grow your own basil for this – the shop-bought kind never seems to have enough punch. When we had the Horn of Plenty, I kept mine in grow-bags in the greenhouse. Now I have a less ambitious garden, so I have to keep them on the step in front of the French windows. The result is the same – very enthusiastic basil.*

In a saucepan, sweat the vegetables in the oil with the bouquet garni for 5 minutes. Do not brown. Add the wine and reduce until almost all the liquid has gone.

Add 150ml/¼ pint of the fish stock and either liquidize or force as much as possible through a sieve.

Return to the pan and then add the rest of the stock. Boil to reduce to about 1.1 litres/2 pints.

While it is reducing, make the pesto sauce: liquidize the parsley, basil (reserving a few sprigs for garnish), pine nuts and garlic in enough oil to result in a purée. Turn it out into a bowl and add just enough cheese to produce a stiff mixture. Season.

Just before serving, spoon the pesto sauce into the centre of each bowl of soup and garnish with the reserved basil sprigs.

1 carrot, peeled and sliced

2 tomatoes, chopped

1 onion, sliced

4 tablespoons olive oil

bouquet garni

150ml/¼ pint white wine

1.1-1.75 litres/2-3 pints fish stock (page 183), according to strength

salt and freshly ground black pepper

*for the pesto sauce:*
115g/4oz fresh basil, or 50g/2oz each parsley and basil

1 tablespoon pine nuts

1 garlic clove

125ml/4fl oz olive oil

115g/4oz grated Parmesan cheese, or more to thicken

# Red Wine Ragout of Fish

OPTIONS

*Cod, halibut, monkfish, swordfish,*
*tuna, turbot*

900g/2lb thick fillets of round fish,
or 1.25kg/2½ lb cutlets

1 onion

1 carrot

2 tomatoes

1 celery stalk

30g/1oz mushroom stalks

5 tablespoons olive oil

1 tablespoon flour

600ml/1 pint fish stock (page 183)

600ml/1 pint chicken stock (or more
fish stock for vegetarians)

1 bouquet garni

3 shallots

200ml/7fl oz red wine

salt and freshly ground black pepper

thyme sprigs, to garnish (optional)

*Whoever said that red wine and fish don't mix? This recipe proves the contrary — and do go ahead and drink a red wine with it to compound the sin! I've found this ragout is terrifically popular with the sort of vegetarians who make fish an exception to their vegetarian rule.*

To make the brown base: chop the onion, carrot, tomatoes and mushroom stalks and brown them in 1 tablespoon of the oil. This will take some time as tomatoes have a lot of liquid in them, about 15-20 minutes.

In a small pan, brown the flour in 1 tablespoon of the oil. Add this mixture to the vegetables with all the stock(s). Bring to the boil and add the bouquet garni. Simmer for about an hour, strain and reserve the resulting brown sauce.

Cut the fish into large chunks or slice it into cutlets, and fry gently in the remaining oil in a pan to stiffen them a little. Remove from the pan with a slotted spoon and keep warm.

Add the shallots with the red wine and boil down until syrupy. Then add the brown sauce base, season and simmer for 10 minutes. Strain out the shallots, if you prefer.

Return the fish to the pan with the sauce. Simmer for a further 5 minutes, until the pieces of fish are thoroughly cooked and any bones will come free easily. Adjust the seasoning, if necessary.

Serve garnished with thyme sprigs, if you wish, and accompanied by button mushrooms sautéed in a little butter and glazed baby onions.

# Tuna Fish in Red Wine

6 tuna steaks, each weighing about 175g/6oz

175ml/6fl oz olive oil

2 onions, thinly sliced

2 garlic cloves, crushed

2 carrots, sliced

½ teaspoon dried thyme

1 bay leaf

sprinkling of dried rosemary

some parsley stalks

4 tomatoes, chopped

2 teaspoons tomato paste

6 black peppercorns

300ml/½ pint full-flavoured red wine

45g/1½ oz flour

about 1.75 litres/3 pints fish stock (page 183)

salt and freshly ground black pepper

*I have cooked this dish for a non-meat-eater while everyone else was having the same thing with beef and nobody knew until the guest spilled the beans and then they all wanted it too! It was very popular. The main difference is that fish needs very little cooking, unlike stewing beef. Even the vegetables take longer than fish so they have to be cooked first.*

Heat one-third of the olive oil in a large pan and throw in the onions, garlic and carrots. Let them take on a good brown colour.

Add in the herbs, tomatoes, tomato paste, peppercorns and wine. Boil off all the liquid until the mixture nearly begins to fry again. This takes a long time but don't give up as you must get rid of the wine esters that make the dish bitter and unpleasantly 'winey'. (Wine is a flavouring to be used like a large squeeze of lemon juice and not a substitute for stock.) Now add the fish stock and bring it to the boil. Simmer for half an hour.

Meanwhile in a small pan, mix half of the remaining olive oil with the flour and cook gently until the flour browns. Stir this well into the simmering vegetables and simmer for another half an hour, topping up with more stock or water as necessary. Strain all the liquid through a large sieve but don't push the vegetables through as well, just give them a good shake and pour a little water over them to rinse off any good juice still clinging.

Rinse out the pan briefly and pour the red wine sauce back and reduce to 450ml/¾ pint. Season with salt and lots of pepper.

In a frying pan, heat the rest of the olive oil until quite hot and sear both sides of the fish steaks, which have been judiciously seasoned. Lift them into the sauce and finish by cooking gently for about 15 minutes (until the centre bone is free). If they make the sauce a bit watery, pour it off and boil it separately until it is a good consistency again.

Serve with mashed potato and green beans just like beef!

# Red Mullet and Bass in Red Wine

*When bass and red mullet have been scaled, the skins shine with colour – brilliant red and silver. Placed alternately on plates, they look quite stunning.*

Peel the baby onions and cook them whole in boiling salted water until tender. Drain and toss them in the butter and sugar over a moderate heat until caramelized. Add the vinegar and boil it away to a syrup. Keep warm.

Boil the salsify in salted water until tender. Peel and slice them into 3cm/1in lengths. Keep warm.

Fry the mushrooms lightly in the oil and season. Keep warm.

Make the sauce: in a saucepan, cook the shallots in 30g/1oz of butter until they brown lightly, Add the wine and boil away until the mixture is syrupy. Add the stocks and boil down to 300ml/½ pint. Beat in 175g/6oz of the remaining butter, reheating the sauce gently as you go. Season and strain.

Flash-fry the pieces of red mullet and bass on both sides in the last of the butter. Cover and leave for 1 minute to finish cooking.

Pour the sauce on 6 warmed plates and arrange the fish on top. Garnish with the prepared vegetables.

675g/1½lb bass fillet, scaled and cut into 3cm/1¼ in portions

675g/1½lb red mullet fillet, scaled and cut into 3cm/1¼ in portions

225g/8oz baby onions

55-85g/2-3oz butter

1 teaspoon sugar

2 tablespoon red wine vinegar

2 salsify roots

50g/2oz horn of plenty mushrooms

1 teaspoon groundnut oil

salt and freshly ground black pepper

*for the sauce:*
4 shallots, finely chopped

225g/8oz unsalted butter

300ml/½ pint red wine

300ml/½ pint fish stock (page 183)

300ml/½ pint chicken stock

# Thai Fish Stew

1 monkfish tail,
sliced into 2.5cm/1in medallions
(about 350g/12oz in total)

6 tiger prawns, peeled and
sliced in half lengthwise

350g/12oz fresh queen scallops

500ml/16fl oz fish stock (page 183)

3 red Thai chillies, sliced

2.5cm/1in piece of fresh root ginger,
grated

3 stalks of lemon grass,
sliced lengthwise

6 spring onions,
sliced diagonally

salt and freshly ground black pepper

torn leaves from 1 bunch
of fresh coriander, to garnish

*I very much enjoy the clear true flavours of Thai cooking. Start with a Thai-style stock if you like, but I always use my everyday fish stock.*

In a large pan, bring the fish stock to the boil, add the chillies, ginger and lemon grass, and simmer gently for 10 minutes to allow the flavours to infuse. Season to taste.

Add the monkfish and spring onions and poach gently for 1 minute. Add the prawns and poach for 20 seconds more. Stir in the scallops, which will stiffen in about 5 seconds. Do not allow the liquid to boil at any time, but just have it hot enough to poach the fish.

Remove the lemon grass and serve immediately in wide soup bowls, scattered with the torn coriander leaves.

# Curried Cream Fish Ragout

*Although this sauce does contain a teaspoon of hot curry paste, there's more to the flavouring than that. The flavour extracted from the shrimp shells gives it character. The Thai rice is very important as it takes away any over-rich effect. You can use flat fish rolled up or cutlets of round fish for this dish, but it must be white, not smoked or pink.*

Melt the butter in a frying pan over a high heat and stiffen the pieces of fish in it. Season well, lift out of the pan with a slotted spoon and keep warm.

Gently fry the onions, thyme and bay leaf in the butter, adding a bit more if some has been absorbed by the fish. Cook until soft, about 10 or 15 minutes.

Meanwhile, peel the shrimps and boil up the shells in just enough water to cover. Strain and reduce to 1 tablespoon.

When the onion is soft add the curry paste to the pan and simmer for a minute, then add the reduced shrimp stock and the cream. Boil up to produce a sauce with a coating consistency and return the white fish to the pan. Simmer together to amalgamate the flavours. Season with a little nutmeg.

Add the cooked shrimps and serve in the centre of a ring of the warm Thai fragrant rice.

OPTIONS
*Haddock, halibut, monkfish, tuna*

675g/1½lb firm white fish fillets or cutlets

about 50g/2oz butter

2 medium onions, chopped

2 teaspoons fresh thyme leaves

bay leaf

115g/4oz freshly cooked shrimps

1 teaspoon hot curry paste

115g/4oz double cream

freshly grated nutmeg to taste

salt and freshly ground black pepper

350g/12oz Thai fragrant rice, boiled or steamed, to serve

# Fish and Vegetable Curry

OPTIONS

*Cod, coley, haddock, halibut, monkfish, pollack, rock salmon, swordfish, squid*

500g/18oz fish chosen from a selection of the options, skinned and filleted as appropriate.

900g/2lb potatoes, cut into chunks

175ml/6fl oz grapeseed or groundnut oil

2 medium onions finely chopped

2 garlic cloves, chopped

5cm/2in piece of fresh ginger, peeled and chopped

2 tablespoons ground cumin

2 tablespoons ground turmeric

2 teaspoons chilli powder

6 ripe tomatoes, coarsely chopped

6 okra, sliced

85g/3oz block of creamed coconut

1 tablespoon chopped leaf coriander

salt and freshly ground black pepper

*This is an ideal sort of dish — bags of interesting things and easy to adapt to available ingredients. I am sure everyone will alter the quantity of chilli or spices to fit their own individual taste, but the combination of flavours is very satisfying.*

Cook the potatoes in boiling salted water until tender, drain and allow to cool.

In half the oil and 2 tablespoons water cook together the onion, garlic and ginger until they have softened.

Increase the heat and boil off any remaining water. Add the rest of the oil and all the spices. Stir well to fry the spices lightly until aromatic. Add the tomatoes and okra. Season and cook over a high heat to dry them out.

Throw in the potato chunks and finally the fish, adding just enough fish stock to moisten it all. Season, cover and simmer for 5 minutes, or until the fish is firm. Add the creamed coconut and let it melt in. Adjust the seasoning if necessary.

Stir in the coriander to serve.

# Fish Croquettes

*Croquettes ought to be easy to make and so they are, provided one knows where the pitfalls are:*

1. *If there isn't enough coating, the croquette will break apart.*
2. *If the ends aren't coated, the mixture will ooze out.*
3. *If the mixture isn't cold enough, it will be impossible to coat it in crumbs.*
4. *If the croquettes are left too long in the oil, they will boil and burst!*
5. *With a really chilled or even frozen croquette the centre may not have heated through by the time the outside is cooked.*

*In view of all this its a wonder anyone ever makes them. There is always the ruse of adding a little mashed potato to the mix, which makes it less runny but still light and much more stable.*

Pour the milk into a pan, add the onion, herbs and spices and bring to the boil. Turn off the heat and leave for half an hour to infuse.

In a large pan, melt the butter, then stir in the flour and cook for a minute. Strain in the flavoured milk and cook, stirring constantly until it forms a thick smooth white sauce. Season it with anchovy essence, salt and pepper. Pour into a non-stick Swiss roll tin or oblong baking tin and leave to cool. Stir in the flaked fish and put the mixture in the freezer for an hour.

Divide the chilled mixture into 12 'fingers', about 6cm/2¼ in long and roll into cork shapes. Put some flour in a shallow bowl and season it, put the lightly beaten egg in a second bowl and the breadcrumbs in a third. Coat the croquettes first in flour, then roll in egg and finally in breadcrumbs, shaking off excess each time. Be sure to pat coating on the ends. Chill again until just beginning to freeze.

Deep-fry the croquettes in very hot oil in batches until golden brown. Keep them hot in a moderate oven until all are cooked.

Serve with a hollandaise sauce (page 184) or just melted butter and lemon juice.

OPTIONS
*Any fish*

300ml/½ pint milk

1 onion, chopped

1 bay leaf

sprig of fresh thyme

freshly grated nutmeg to taste

3 cloves

50g/2oz butter

50g/2oz flour, plus more for coating

2 teaspoons anchovy essence

350g/12oz cooked fish, flaked or chopped

2 eggs

115g/4oz fresh breadcrumbs

salt and freshly ground black pepper

grapeseed or groundnut oil, for deep-frying

hollandaise sauce (page 184) or melted butter and lemon juice to serve

# Fish and Potato Pie

OPTIONS

*Cod, haddock, halibut, hake, whiting*

450g/1lb cooked mixed fish, flaked

900g/2lb (not too floury) potatoes

125ml/4fl oz medium-dry white wine

175g/6oz butter

1½ tablespoon flour

400ml/14fl oz milk

freshly grated nutmeg to taste

30g/1oz Parmesan cheese

2 teaspoons Dijon mustard

175g/6oz mushrooms, sliced

½ teaspoon lemon juice

2 or 3 spring onions

2 tablespoons chopped parsley

50g/2oz grated Cheddar cheese

salt and freshly ground black pepper

*Its name doesn't do this dish justice. It looks good, with the overlapping cheesy-brown potato topping, and tastes as good as it looks! I've made it with all kinds of fish and it always works. Make sure the sauce is thick before you add the fish as it is certain to thin it a bit by oozing out some of its juices as it reheats.*

Peel the potatoes, slice them thickly and boil in salted water until tender. Drain.

In a large saucepan, reduce the wine with 50g/2oz butter until there is much more butter than wine. Stir in the flour and cook briefly, stirring. Then add the milk and cook to a thick white sauce. Season with salt, pepper, nutmeg, Parmesan cheese and mustard.

In a frying pan, sauté the sliced mushrooms in 50g/2oz of the butter. Season. Mix the lemon juice with 1 tablespoon water and pour this over the mushrooms. Simmer to reduce until the mushrooms begin to fry, but do not let them brown.

Mix the mushrooms with the fish and fold these into the sauce. Thin out with a little extra milk, if necessary. Add the chopped parsley and turn it all into a shallow pie dish.

In the frying pan, sauté the potatoes in the rest of the butter until they begin to brown. Add the spring onions and remove from the heat.

Preheat a hot grill. Carefully lay the potato slices, overlapping, on top of the fish. Pour over the rest of the butter with the spring onions and sprinkle with the Cheddar. Brown under the grill.

# Crêpes Soufflés

*Next time you poach some smoked fish, cook it in a mixture of equal parts milk and water, then save the resulting stock for this dish. It makes an interesting smoky-flavoured sauce with which to bind the fish.*

Preheat the oven to 250°C/475°F/gas9 and oil a baking sheet or line it with non-stick parchment.

Melt 50g/2oz of the butter in a saucepan, stir in the flour and cook this roux briefly. Then add the milk and fish water. Cook, stirring continuously, to a thick smooth sauce. Remove from the heat and stir in the egg yolks. Season.

Whisk the egg whites until firm. Stir a large spoonful into the sauce to loosen it and then gently fold in the rest.

Warm the cooked fish in the remaining butter with seasoning to taste. Lay the pancakes flat. Place 30g/1oz of fish on one half of each pancake and spread with the soufflé mix. Fold the other half over and place on the baking sheet. Repeat with the remaining fish, pancakes and soufflé mixture. Cook in the hot oven until risen.

Lift out gently and serve on hot plates. Eat immediately!

OPTIONS
*Cod, haddock, hake, mackerel, salmon*

350g/12oz flaked cooked fish

115g/4oz butter

40g/1½ oz flour

300ml/½ pint milk or equal parts milk and smoked fish cooking water (see above)

2 eggs, separated, plus whites of 2 more eggs

6 pancakes, (cooked as described on page 48)

salt and freshly ground black pepper

grapeseed or groundnut oil for greasing (optional)

# Fish Timbales with Spinach

OPTIONS

*Haddock, halibut, sole (pictured), turbot*

550g/1¼ lb fresh leaf spinach

2 egg yolks

115g/4oz raw fish

75g/2½ oz whipping cream

freshly grated nutmeg to taste

salt and freshly ground black pepper

sauce beurre blanc (page 185)
or hot crème fraîche, to serve

sprigs of parsley or chervil,
to garnish (optional)

*These 'timbales', savoury mixtures cooked in a mould and turned out, can be reheated very successfully so long as you don't overcook them (they soufflé and then collapse, so the texture is ruined). Replace the spinach with cooked leeks or broccoli for a change, but squeeze them well to remove excess moisture before mixing them in.*

Preheat the oven to 110°C/230°F/gas¼. Cook the spinach in boiling salted water, drain and squeeze quite dry in a cloth. Weigh out exactly 200g/7oz.

In a blender or food processor, liquidize the fish with the egg yolks. Add the spinach and nutmeg and purée until smooth. Add the cream and mix briefly to incorporate.

Butter 6 individual 150ml/¼ pint savarin moulds and divide the mixture between them (or just fill one large savarin mould).

Place in a bain-marie or roasting pan lined with wet newspaper and half-filled with hot water. Cook in the oven for 45 minutes until set.

Turn out by placing each mould on a plate and giving it a shake. Garnish with herb sprigs, if you like, and serve with a beurre blanc or hot crème fraîche.

# Pasta Bound with Fish and Cream

OPTIONS
*Cod, haddock, smoked haddock,*
*clams, prawns, squid*

675g/1½ lb mixed fish,
free of skin, bone and shell

1kg/2¼ lb fresh or
675g/1¼ lb dried pasta

30g/1 oz butter

1 medium onion, finely chopped

150ml/¼ pint white wine
or Noilly Prat white vermouth

bay leaf

300ml/½ pint fish stock
(page 183)

300ml/½ pint double cream

1 egg yolk

50g/2oz Parmesan cheese,
finely grated

salt and freshly ground black pepper

*Spaghetti carbonara is a very well known Italian dish with cream, mushrooms and bacon. If you substitute fish for the bacon the whole effect changes, although the technique remains the same.*

Cook the pasta in lots of rapidly boiling salted water until just tender. Drain.

While the pasta is cooking, melt the butter in a saucepan with 3 tablespoons of water and sweat the onion in it until soft, but do not allow to brown. Add the wine and bay leaf and reduce until the butter appears again. Add the stock.

Poach the fish in this stock and wine reduction until firm and then drain, retaining the stock. Keep the cooked fish warm.

Add the cream to the stock and boil down to 450ml/¾ pint. Beat in the egg yolk and season.

Fold in the drained poached fish and mix it all with the pasta. Adjust seasoning, being generous with the pepper. Finally, sprinkle it with Parmesan.

# Fresh Tagliarini Verde with Fish and Cheese Sauce

*The fish to use for this dish must be both moist and flavourful. I favour salmon and bass to give me the combination I look for, but I am sure you will find others. The fennel adds texture.*

Preheat the oven to 250°C/475°F/gas9.

Slice the fennel into chunks and cook it in a very little lightly salted water (2-3 tablespoons) with 50g/2oz of the butter, until tender but not mushy.

At the same time, cook the pasta in lots of rapidly boiling salted water until just al dente. Drain and mix with 85g/3oz of the butter.

At the same time also steam the fish over boiling water until firm. Drain well if necessary.

While the pasta and fish are cooking, make a cheese sauce: in a saucepan, melt the remaining butter and blend in the flour. Cook for a minute, stirring all the time. Whisk in the milk and simmer, stirring, for 5 minutes until it is a thick smooth sauce. Stir in the Parmesan and season.

Add the fish to the spaghetti, together with the fennel and chopped parsley. Spread evenly in a large ovenproof dish or 6 individual shallow ovenproof bowls.

Pour the sauce over the pasta and fish, sprinkle with the Cheddar and brown in the oven for about 20 minutes.

## Options

*Bass, cod, coley, haddock, halibut, monkfish, pollack, rock salmon, salmon, swordfish, squid*

350g/12oz salmon, skinned and filleted

350g/12oz bass, skinned and filleted

2 fennel bulbs

200g/7oz butter

350g/12oz fresh tagliarini verde

40g/1½oz flour

300ml/½ pint milk

115g/4oz Parmesan cheese, grated

1 tablespoon chopped flat-leaved parsley

115g/4oz Cheddar cheese, grated

salt and freshly ground black pepper

# Hot Baked Fish Pudding

*This classic English dish makes a good family-style main course. It looks very pretty made with salmon but other fish will do just as well. It can be served with a thin parsley sauce, sauce beurre blanc or hollandaise flavoured with a little reduced Noilly Prat.*

Preheat the oven to 110°C/230°F/gas¼.

Make the binding mixture: melt the butter in a small frying pan and cook the onions in it until lightly browned.

In a blender or food processor, purée the raw fish with the eggs. Add the cream and breadcrumbs and blend a little longer. Turn out into a bowl, stir in the onions and season.

Line an ovenproof bowl first with film and then with the blanched leek leaves, radiating from the centre outwards like the spokes of a wheel and slightly overlapping, with the ends overhanging the edge. Fill the bowl with layers of the binding mix and the cooked fish, starting and ending with the binding mix. Cover with leek leaves, bring up the overhangs to seal the edges, and then cover with film.

Cook in a bain-marie or roasting pan lined with wet newspaper and half-filled with hot water in the oven for 1¼ hours, or until the centre of the top is firm and cooked.

Serve with a thin parsley sauce or, for a more special occasion, with beurre blanc, or just butter and stock boiled together with Noilly Prat white vermouth.

OPTIONS
*Salmon and Cod (pictured), John Dory, plaice, soles*

450g/1lb lightly cooked skinless, boneless fish pieces, flaked

*for the binding mixture*
350g/12oz raw white fish, free of skin and bones

whites of 4 egg whites
or 3 whole eggs

2 tablespoons cream

2 onions, finely chopped

50g/2oz butter

green leaves of 2 leeks, blanched

salt and freshly ground black pepper

thin parsley sauce (page 185), sauce beurre blanc (page 185) or hollandaise sauce (page 184) flavoured with a little reduced Noilly Prat

# Spanish Fish Omelette

OPTIONS
*Cod, hake, mussels, tuna,
swordfish, prawns*

500g/1lb 2oz raw mixed fish

1 large Spanish onion, sliced

4 tablespoons olive oil

3 medium potatoes, parboiled and
thickly sliced

½ teaspoon paprika

6 eggs

salt and freshly ground black pepper

*This makes quite a substantial light lunch dish and is one of those great standbys for a hungry family. Choose an interesting selection for the fish content, say 3 prawns cut in half, 6 small pieces of tuna, 6 small pieces of hake and a few mussels.*

Fry the onion in half the oil until lightly browned. Fry the potatoes with the onion until they brown and are quite cooked. Don't worry if they break up a bit.

Add the rest of the oil then the fish, starting with the larger pieces and fry them until they are nearly cooked. Sprinkle with the paprika.

Beat the eggs in a separate bowl and season. Stir them into the onion, potato and fish mixture and then allow them to cook undisturbed over a moderate heat until set on top.

Turn the mixture over out on to a large platter, divide into portions and eat as a snack or light lunch.

# Fish Risotto with Parmesan

*Don't be tempted to cook the rice from raw in the fish stock, as the natural gelatine that has come from the fish bones will prevent the rice from swelling and absorbing the liquid, so it will remain hard. When the rice has parboiled and begun to swell, then it will cook in the stock. To compensate for this, however, the stock is first concentrated to make up for the water that the rice has already absorbed.*

First boil the fish stock to reduce it to half its volume. At the same time parboil the rice in salted water until nearly tender. Drain.

Meanwhile, cook the onion in 50g/2oz of the butter and 3 tablespoons of water, boiling the water away it until the butter starts to fry the onion and brown it. Add the sage, thyme and white wine. Boil off the wine and add the concentrated fish stock.

Cut the fish into small pieces and add these (and the mussels in their shells if you are using them) to the onion mixture. Put the nearly cooked rice on top and cover with a lid. Cook gently until the rice has absorbed the stock, turning the mixture over gently a couple of times.

Finish by mixing in the Parmesan and the remaining butter. Check the seasoning, adding generous amounts of pepper.

OPTIONS
*Cod, coley, halibut, monkfish, salmon, turbot, mussels, prawns, squid*

550g/1¼ lb long-grain rice (NOT risotto rice)

450g/1lb raw mixed fish, free of bones and skin

12 mussels, scrubbed and cleaned (optional)

1.1 litres/2 pints fish stock (page 183)

1 onion, finely chopped

115g/4oz butter

½ teaspoon chopped fresh sage

½ teaspoon dried thyme

150ml/¼ pint white wine

50g/2oz Parmesan cheese, grated

salt and freshly ground black pepper

# Fruits de Mer en Croustade

OPTIONS

*Sole, scallops (pictured), crawfish,*
*lobster, John Dory, lemon sole,*
*slip sole,*

16 small skinned slip sole fillets

550g/1¼ lb puff pastry

1 egg yolk

8 scallops

1 whole crawfish, weighing about
350g/12oz, boiled

115g/4oz butter

150ml/¼ pint white wine or Noilly
Prat vermouth

300ml/½ pint fish stock (page 183)

300ml/½ pint whipping cream

40g/1½ oz flour

salt and freshly ground black pepper

*This recipe is a traditional French dish using only three different fish. There's no reason why you can't vary them, but don't let it become a dustbin for any oddments you have around! The slip soles recommended here weigh 225g/8oz at most, so the fillets are very small and neat.*

Preheat the oven to 250°C/475°F/gas9.

Roll the pastry out into 2 rectangles about 23.5x15cm/9x6in. Place them on top of each other and trim them neatly. Cut into six 7.5cm/3x3in squares. Then take the top layers of each square and cut an inner square out of each one, leaving a 1cm/½in border. Reserve these inner squares for 'lids' and score them with diagonal slashes. Make a glaze by mixing egg yolk with a little water and brush the bottom squares lightly with it, being careful not to let the wash drip down the sides or the pastry won't rise properly. Press the top border layers back in place. If you like, twist the corners before replacing them to produce the effect in the photograph. Paint the tops of each of the croustades and the reserved 'lids' with the wash. Arrange the cases and lids separately on baking sheets and bake for 20-25 minutes, until well risen and golden brown.

While they are cooking, melt 30g/1oz of the butter in a small pan, add the wine and reduce to 1 tablespoon.

Roll the sole fillets and poach them gently in the fish stock enriched with the wine reduction until firm.

Slice the scallops in half into two thin discs, and add to the sole to heat up gently, but do not allow to boil. Remove the meat from the crawfish.

Drain off the stock into a small pan and reduce it to 300ml/½ pint. Add the cream.

Make a roux by melting 50g/2oz butter in a large saucepan and stirring in the flour. Cook the mixture briefly and then stir in the reduced stock and cream mixture. Simmer, stirring, for a few

minutes to produce a smooth thick velvety velouté sauce. Season and add the juices from the fish.

Heat up the slices of crawfish in the remaining butter and fold them into the sauce with the fish. Warm through thoroughly but gently.

Remove and discard any soft dough in the centres of the pastry cases, spoon the fruits de mer mixture into them and top with the 'lids' at a jaunty angle if you like.

# Mère Brazier Quenelles

OPTIONS
*Haddock, pike,
salmon, sole*

175g/6oz raw haddock fillets,
skin removed

9 eggs

175g/6oz butter

freshly grated nutmeg to taste

salt and freshly ground black pepper

Saffron soup (page 64), or sauce
Américaine (page 186) thinned with
a little reduced fish stock

*for the panada:*
250ml/8fl oz milk

30g/1oz butter

225g/8oz flour

*Until you have eaten these quenelles you haven't lived! The quenelles of La Mère Brazier, one of the very greatest of the Michelin three-star chefs in the 1950s to 70s, were a legend in her time. Having lunched at her restaurant on the Col de la Luère near Lyons one day, I had the temerity to ask her to explain the difference between her quenelles (which were light compared to the quenelles Lyonnais, which could be like lead) and mine — which were quenelles only in shape and were really a mousseline of cream, fish and eggs. The result was two glorious days in her kitchen where she first tested me to see if I was serious and then laboriously took me step by step through the procedure of making quenelles for 60.*

*She had no blenders or mixers, so this involved boning the fish (pike or brochet), mincing it and the panada, and forcing the purée through a sieve to get rid of stray filaments. It took two days, since drying the panada in the oven was an overnight operation!*

*We are spoiled rotten now. This recipe has been scaled down to today's proportions, using today's machines. Best of luck!*

Preheat the oven to 250°C/475°F/gas9 and put a large pan of salted water on to boil.

Make the panada (you will not be strong enough to mix it

# Tricolor Hot Terrine

*This highly decorative layered terrine is a real show-stopper and it tastes good too. If you don't want to layer it you can simply marble the colours through one another.*

Preheat the oven to 110°C/230°F/gas¼.

In a heavy-based saucepan, melt the butter and gently cook the onion in it until softened. Then add the wine and fish stock together with some seasoning. Reduce until the mixture measures about 150ml/¼ pint.

In a blender or food processor, purée together the fish, egg whites, salt to taste and the wine reduction. Add the soft breadcrumbs a spoonful or two at a time until the mixture only just barely turns in the goblet.

Divide the mixture between three bowls. Stir 2 tablespoons of the cream into one. Purée the peppers and stir these into the second, together with 1 tablespoon of cream. Stir the spinach and the remaining cream into the third. You should now have 3 distinctively coloured mixtures.

Line an ovenproof 23cm/9in terrine with film. Spread the mixtures in layers in the terrine, with the white one in the middle, or pipe them in like a Battenberg cake. Cover with film and bake in a bain-marie, or in a roasting pan lined with wet newspaper and half-filled with hot water, for about 1 hour until set. Do not allow to overcook (i.e. cook it too long or at too high a temperature) or it will start to soufflé.

Slice and serve hot, with either a light butter sauce (page 185) or simply with cold crème fraîche. To serve cold: allow to cool completely, then chill briefly, turn out and cut into slices.

OPTIONS
*Cod, scallops, halibut (pictured), haddock, rainbow trout, salmon, turbot*

675g/1½ lb boneless skinless white fish

1 onion, chopped

30g/1oz butter

300ml/½ pint white wine

150ml/¼ pint fish stock (page 183)

whites of 8-10 eggs (use the yolks for sauces, cover with a thin layer of water and they keep well in the refrigerator)

85g/3oz soft breadcrumbs

4 tablespoons double cream

½ red sweet pepper, deseeded and roasted over a naked flame until charred all over and then peeled

50g/2oz spinach, cooked

salt and freshly ground black pepper

light butter sauce (page 185) or cold crème fraîche, to serve

# Cold Rice Salad of Mixed Fish

OPTIONS

*Cod, huss, lobster (precooked), prawns,
shrimp, monkfish pieces, smoked eel,
smoked salmon trimmings*

450g/1lb mixed fish (to include,
if possible, some prawns or shrimps
and some smoked fish), boned and
skinned as appropriate

285g/10 oz rice

5 tablespoons olive oil

1 tablespoon raisins

125ml/4fl oz white wine vinegar

freshly grated nutmeg to taste

30g/1oz pine nuts

1 tablespoon ground cumin

1 tablespoon ground coriander

12 cooked mussels, de-bearded
(see page 189)

pared zest of 1 uncoated lemon,
cut into strips

50g/2oz creamed coconut

salt and freshly ground black pepper

chopped fresh coriander, to garnish

*This is a preparation which, although not a course in itself, has
its place in a cold buffet. The sweetness of the raisins come as a
pleasant surprise in an otherwise savoury dish.*

Measure the rice in a measuring jug. In a large heavy-based
saucepan, fry the rice in 2 tablespoons of the olive oil until it
becomes opaque.

Measure out twice the volume of water as rice and add this to
the pan with the raisins and salt. Cover with a lid and gently cook
until all the water has been absorbed by the rice. Remove the lid
and allow to steam for a minute.

Add the vinegar and plenty of nutmeg, pepper and more salt if
necessary. Turn the mixture into a bowl and leave to cool, stirring
from time to time.

Toast the pine nuts by dry-frying them briefly and add them to
the rice mixture.

In a large heavy-based saucepan, lightly fry the ground cumin
and coriander, toss in the prawns, shrimps and the skinned and
boned pieces of white fish, adding more oil as necessary, and cook
them until they are firm.

Add the mussels and lemon zest and bind with the creamed
coconut. Fold this into the rice, together with any smoked pieces
you may wish to add. Allow to cool and then chill.

Serve garnished with chopped fresh coriander.

# Salmon and Trout Rillettes

*Rillettes are a speciality of the Loire, pounded chopped pork with flavourings preserved under a layer of pork fat. This starter is made of chopped fish bound with butter, moulded into a round shape, topped with sour cream and set off with a 'hat band' of smoked salmon. Instead of metal ring moulds I use empty 'topped and tailed' small tomato tins.*

Blend the flaked fish with the shallot and butter until smooth. Add 5 tablespoons of the crème fraîche, nutmeg, lemon juice and seasoning. Chill until quite cold.

Make the dill cream sauce: mix together the cream, chopped dill and enough fish stock to thin it out a little. Add a squeeze of lemon juice if you like it even more tart.

Nearly fill six 7.5cm/3in well oiled ring moulds (or small empty tomato tins, see above) with the chilled fish mixture and top with the remaining crème fraîche mixed with the diced tomato and dill. Remove the rings, wrap ribbons of smoked salmon around the edges and chill again briefly.

Serve really cold, with the dill cream sauce.

350g/12oz lightly poached salmon, skinned, boned and flaked

175g/6oz smoked trout, skinned, boned and flaked

1 shallot, finely chopped

50g/2oz butter, softened

300ml/½ pint crème fraîche

freshly grated nutmeg to taste

½ teaspoon lemon juice

2 tomatoes, skinned, deseeded and diced

1 tablespoon chopped dill

115g/4oz smoked salmon, cut into long ribbons

salt and freshly ground black pepper

*for the dill cream sauce:*
175g/6oz sour cream

1 tablespoon chopped dill

squeeze of lemon juice (optional)

2-3 tablespoons fish stock (page 183)

# Kippers in a Sweet Marinade

OPTIONS
*Smoked haddock, kippers*

6 fresh and moist undyed
smoked kippers

100g/3½ oz sugar

100ml/3½ fl oz mild rice vinegar
or white wine vinegar

2 onions, sliced into rings

100ml/3½ fl oz grapeseed or
groundnut oil (optional)

1 head of Chinese leaves,
coarsely shredded

bunch of watercress

freshly ground black pepper
(optional)

*This makes a most unusual starter as the kippers are eaten raw. The fillets may be sliced into strips then rolled in buttered brown bread and trimmed to form part of a finger buffet, or simply served with raw onion rings as part of an hors d'oeuvre. Here, however, the dish is set out as a salad.*

*As the fish marinates it swaps its own juices for the marinade liquid and becomes progressively drier, which is why it is such a good idea to add oil to the marinade if the fish is to be left in it for longer than 4 hours, as this slows down the drying process. You can use some of the marinade as a vinaigrette for the salad.*

In a bowl, dissolve the sugar in the vinegar and add the onion rings. If you are going to leave the fish to marinate for longer than 4 hours add the oil as well.

Ease the backbones out of the kippers and, with a pair of tweezers, pull out as many bones as possible. Handle the fish gently so that they don't break up. Lay them in the marinade, making sure they are covered with it, and leave in the refrigerator for at least 4 hours or (if you have added oil to the marinade, see above) up to 4 days.

To serve: make a salad with the Chinese leaves and watercress. Cut the kippers into long fingers and lay these over the salad. Garnish with the onions rings and use a little of the marinade to dress the salad. No other seasoning is necessary, although some people add a grating of black pepper.

# Smoked Mackerel Pâté

*Although this preparation has gone out of fashion, it still makes an excellent starter and soon enough the wheel will turn and it will be back in!*

Remove all the bones and skin from the mackerel, place the flesh in a blender with the butter and purée it. Turn it into a bowl and allow to cool a little.

Beat in the cream and add the lemon juice to taste. Season carefully. Allow to cool, but do not chill. Put in a serving bowl.

Serve with parsley, hard boiled-egg and spring onions in little piles on each plate. Serve hot toast separately.

1 smoked mackerel
(whole fish variety, not dried
or peppered brown ones)

225g/8oz unsalted butter, melted

125ml/4fl oz double cream

lemon juice to taste

salt and freshly ground black pepper

*to serve:*
3 tablespoons chopped parsley

2 hard-boiled eggs, chopped

1-2 spring onions, chopped

hot toast

175

# Salt Cod Pâté

900g/2lb salt cod

6 garlic cloves

300ml/½ pint olive oil

300ml/½ pint double cream

juice of 1 lemon

freshly ground black pepper

slices of warm toast, to serve

*This recipe is one from a French regional dinner at our restaurant, though its original source is now forgotten. It uses salt cod, which today is one of the few examples of this type of curing and preserving. It has a unique flavour that some people might find difficult to appreciate the first time they taste it. Like Brie and other smelly cheeses it can be addictive. To my mind it is now an acquired taste, but years ago it was commonplace. Ask your fishmonger for it as you are unlikely to see it displayed on account of its unattractive appearance.*

*The main secret of using it is to have patience while it soaks for about 36 to 48 hours, according to the thickness, to get rid of excess salt. Change the water at least once during this time.*

Soak the fish as explained above. Rinse and place in a large pan of cold water with the garlic. Bring slowly to the boil and continue to cook until the flesh will come away from the bones, about 15 minutes.

Drain the fish, reserving the garlic. Peel that. Discard all the skin and bones and put the fish flesh in a blender or food processor with the garlic pieces. Switch on and feed in the oil a little at a time to purée the fish and make an emulsion.

Add the cream to soften the flavour, then add lemon juice and pepper to taste. Turn it out into a bowl and serve at room temperature with warm toast. Do not chill.

# Millefeuilles of Soft Roes, Cheese Sauce and Spinach

*This rich lunch dish makes a good introduction to soft roes if you're not quite sure you will like them, as the pastry gives a bit of crunch to what would otherwise be a rather soft mouthful.*

Preheat the oven to 190°C/375°/gas5. Roll out the puff pastry very thinly into 2 rectangles about 37.5x30cm/15x12in. Cut each into 18 oblongs, 7.5x10cm/5x4in. Prick all over with a fork and lay on 2 baking sheets. Place another baking sheet on top of each and lightly weight so the pastry will cook flat and crisp without rising. (If you haven't enough baking sheets, work in batches.)

Cook in the oven for about 20 minutes, until crisp all the way through. Remove the top sheets and allow the pastry to cool.

Cook the spinach in boiling salted water, drain and squeeze dry in a cloth. Glisten with 15g/½ oz of the butter.

To make the cheese sauce, melt the remaining butter in a saucepan over a gentle heat and stir in the flour. Cook, stirring, for a few minutes, then add half the milk, stirring, to make a thick paste. Stir in about three-quarters of the remaining milk and cook well until thick and smooth. Adjust consistency with remaining milk if necessary, it should be a fairly thick coating consistency. Stir in all of the Cheddar and half the Parmesan. Season, then cover the pan to keep the steam in and prevent a skin from forming.

Poach the prepared roes in a little lemon-flavoured salted water until firm, about 5 minutes. Drain and fold into the cheese sauce.

Preheat a hot grill. Now build up the dish as follows: arrange 6 rectangles of pastry on a heatproof sheet or tray which will go under the grill to form the bases. Cover these with a layer of spinach, then another rectangle of pastry, then the roes in cheese sauce and top up with a third sheet of pastry. Arrange the Mozzarella slices over the top, sprinkle with the rest of the Parmesan and melt the cheese under the grill, so that it dribbles down the sides. Serve immediately on warmed plates.

675g/1½ lb soft herring roes, prepared as described on page 189

550g/1¼ lb puff pastry

450g/1lb spinach, or 225g/8oz Swiss chard leaves

50g/2oz butter

40g/1½oz flour

300ml/½ pint milk

115g/4oz Cheddar cheese, grated

115g/4oz Parmesan cheese, grated

115g/4oz Mozzarella cheese, thinly sliced

juice of ½ lemon

salt and freshly ground black pepper

# Smoked Cod's Roe Paste

225g/8oz smoked cod's roe

225g/8oz unsalted butter
(or more to taste)

fresh toast, to serve

*for the garnish:*
1 onion, finely chopped

2 hard-boiled eggs, chopped

30g/1oz fresh parsley, chopped

*This very simple and effective mixture (pictured), reminiscent of smoked salmon, is perfect for nibbles or as a first course with the chopped garnishes. Make sure you buy a good smoked cod's roe — it should be soft and moist.*

Slit the cod's roe in half and discard the skin. In a food processor, blend the soft insides with the butter until it is well mixed. If it is still too strong in flavour, add a little more butter.

Serve with fresh toast and the various chopped garnishes.

# Soft Herring Roes

450g/1lb soft herring roes

115g/4oz flour

115g/4oz butter

3 tablespoons grapeseed or
groundnut oil (optional)

salt and freshly ground black pepper

1 tablespoon chopped parsley

hot buttered toast, to serve

3 lemons, quartered, to serve

*This is one of our favourite breakfast dishes — or light lunch or, indeed, snack at any time!*

Rinse the roes quickly under gently running water and pat dry.

Remove the 'string' running along the roes if you want them to stay flat when cooked. Dip them in flour which has been heavily seasoned with salt and pepper (this is something so often required that you might ready-mix a quantity and keep it in a jar).

Melt the butter with the oil (or use just butter) in a frying pan until very hot. Lay the floured roes in the pan and brown on both sides as quickly as you can without burning the butter.

Serve the roes on hot buttered toast, sprinkled with parsley, and accompanied by lemon quarters.

# stocks & sauces

*Good stock or a well made sauce can transform even the most ordinary fish into a flavourful, often sophisticated dish*

# Fish Stock

*Any non-oily fish will make an acceptable stock, but a 'luxury' stock needs well-flavoured fish, such as turbot or Dover sole.*

*The gelatine in fish bones is easily dissolved by boiling and, if you are not careful, produces a revolting fish glue. The secret is to have the liquid barely boiling, then the flavour comes out of the fish but the glue doesn't. Protein starts to cook at 70°C and at 100°C is hard-boiled, so the flavour will be best obtained at just below the boiling point. Unfortunately, vegetables won't cook below boiling point, which is why they are simmered first to make sure that they have given up their flavour before cooking the fish at the lower temperature.*

*The bones will also break down if they are cooked for too long, so unusually in the making of stock there is no virtue in allowing the cooking to go on for longer than the prescribed 30 minutes — indeed cook it any longer and it will start to get bitter.*

1 onion, coarsely chopped

1 leek, coarsely chopped

1 celery stalk, coarsely chopped

1 small head of fennel, coarsely chopped

few sprigs of thyme

1-2 bay leaves

6-10 black peppercorns

150ml/¼ pint white wine

2.25kg/5lb white fish trimmings (ideally including a cod's head)

Simmer the vegetable and other aromatic flavourings in just enough water to cover until the vegetables are soft, about 20 minutes. Add the white wine and boil to reduce by half.

Meanwhile, clean the fish trimmings of roes and blood, cutting them out if necessary. In the case of a large fish head, use scissors to remove the gills and rinse the head out. Press the trimmings into the pan with the vegetables and cover with cold water.

Slowly bring just up to the boil, lower the heat so that the water remains just below the boil and simmer gently for 30 minutes.

Allow to cool. Strain and allow to settle. Pour off the top of the stock and reduce it down to a concentrate.

This enriched stock may be frozen in 300ml/½ pint pots.

## Court-bouillon

*Court-bouillon is used as the medium for poaching what would otherwise be a dull-tasting fish. Consequently, a court-bouillon is rarely used to make a sauce as it has too strong a flavour of its own.*

1.1 litres/2 pints water

200ml/7fl oz white wine vinegar

2 onions, coarsely chopped

2 celery stalks

10 parsley stalks

10 black peppercorns, crushed

1 bay leaf

1 sprig of thyme

Put all the ingredients in a large pan, bring to the boil and simmer for half and hour. Season, strain and use or allow to cool.

## Mayonnaise

*Mayonnaise goes well with almost any cold poached fish – and with any accompanying vegetables or salads.*

*Always add some salt to the egg yolks when you start making mayonnaise as this gives it time to dissolve before the oil is incorporated. The trick in making mayonnaise it is to whisk the egg yolks until they are pale (about 5 minutes in a machine) before adding any mustard or oil, which can then be added much more easily. Grapeseed oil produces a very light mayonnaise.*

2 egg yolks

¼ teaspoon salt

300ml/½ pint grapeseed oil

2 teaspoon Dijon mustard, or more to taste

1 tablespoons white wine vinegar

In a medium-sized bowl, beat the egg yolks with the salt until pale. Stir in the mustard.

Now feed in the oil a spoonful at a time, beating well until it is all incorporated and the mayonnaise is thick and smooth.

Thin out with the vinegar and water as necessary.

## Hollandaise Sauce

*This is one of the most sophisticated of sauces and has many applications. It can make the plainest of dishes seem quite luxurious.*

450g/1lb unsalted butter, melted

2 shallots, finely chopped

10 black peppercorns, crushed

300ml/½ pint white wine vinegar

150ml/¼ pint white wine

4 egg yolks

salt and freshly ground black pepper

Put 50g/2oz of the butter in a heavy-based saucepan over a gentle heat. Cook the shallots with the peppercorns in the butter until they are soft but not brown.

Add the wine and vinegar and boil to reduce until syrupy. Add 150ml/¼ pint of water and boil vigorously for 1 minute.

Strain, pressing as much flavour as possible out of the shallots, which can now be discarded. Boil the resulting liquid down to about 4 teaspoons.

Place the egg yolks in a liquidizer and add the 4 teaspoons of vinegar/shallot essence. Feed in the remaining hot melted butter gradually until it is well incorporated and the sauce is thick and smooth. Season.

## Sauce Beurre Blanc

*This sauce is like a light hollandaise (opposite) and it goes well with any hot white fish.*

2 shallots, finely chopped

150ml/¼ pint white wine

225g/8oz unsalted butter

1 tablespoon double cream

salt and freshly ground black pepper

Put the shallots and wine together in a pan with ½ teaspoon butter and boil until it is nearly dry.

Add the cream and boil until the mixture thickens. Beat in the remaining butter, little by little, allowing the sauce nearly to boil each time but not quite. Season to taste and strain.

## Gastrique

*This is an acid sauce base made by reducing wine and/or vinegar to a concentrated essence. The flavour is enhanced by simmering shallots and peppercorns with it during reduction. It is used when the cook doesn't want the flavour of other acids like lemon juice to clash with an accompanying wine.*

1 teaspoon oil

2 shallots, finely chopped

300ml/½ pint wine or wine vinegar

Soften shallots by cooking them for 1 minute in the oil, but do not allow them to brown.

Add the wine or vinegar and reduce until the fluid has been absorbed by the shallots. Add 150ml/¼ pint of water and boil fiercely for 2 minutes.

Strain, pressing as much flavour out of the shallots as possible. Reduce this down to about a tablespoon of liquid.

Use immediately or store in a screw-top bottle in the refrigerator.

## Light Butter Sauce

*This quick and easy-to-make sauce is almost universal in its applications and can use the juices from cooking to advantage.*

250ml/8fl oz stock

225g/8 oz unsalted butter

1 shallot, finely chopped

3 tablespoons white wine

salt and freshly ground black pepper

In a heavy-based saucepan, melt one-quarter of the butter and simmer the shallots in it for 1 minute.

Add the wine and reduce to a syrup. Add the stock, beat in the butter and boil together until they emulsify lightly.

Strain and season. Be prepared to beat in a little hot water if the sauces seems to be 'oiling'.

## Parsley Sauce

*This is possibly the most traditional sauce to serve with fish in this country. This method is particularly simple if you have a food processor, and delivers a wonderfully coloured and potently flavoured sauce.*

125g/4½oz parsley

575ml/1 pint milk

85g/3oz butter, melted

50g/2oz flour

salt and freshly ground black pepper

Tear the leaves off the parsley stalks and crush the stalks with a meat mallet. Place the crushed stalks in a pan with the milk, bring to the boiling point and remove from the heat. Set aside in a warm place.

Remove the parsley stalks from the milk and pour it into a blender. Add the parsley leaves and liquidize until the milk is bright green and the parsley leaves are chopped. With the machine still running, pour in the melted butter and add the flour. Empty it all into a saucepan and bring to the boil quickly, stirring until thickened and smooth. Season.

## Tomato Sauce

*This basic tomato sauce goes well with many fish dishes and can also serve as a dressing for pasta.*

3 tablespoons olive oil

1 onion, chopped

1 garlic clove, crushed

150 ml/¼ pint white wine

675g/1½lb tomatoes, skinned and deseeded

150 ml/¼ pint fish stock (see page 183)

2 teaspoons tomato paste

½ tablespoon fresh marjoram,
   plus more to garnish

½ teaspoon dried thyme

salt and freshly ground black pepper

Heat the oil in a large saucepan and cook the onion in it briefly until just softened. Add the garlic and cook that, allowing it to brown a little.

Add the wine and tomatoes and cook, pulping them down until they start to fry.

Add the fish stock or white wine blended with the tomato paste and the herbs. Bring to the boil and simmer gently for 10 minutes. Season to taste.

## Sauce Américaine

*This shellfish sauce is used to dress white fish and can transform a very ordinary fish into a special occasion treat. If you can possibly get hold of it, some added lobster butter makes an enormous difference to the flavour of this sauce. This may either be a preparation made from butter flavoured with cooked lobster shells, or it could be butter beaten with lobster coral as described on page 106 which gives colour.*

2 onions

2 carrots

4 tomatoes

1 celery stalk

30g/1oz mushroom trimmings

3 tablespoons grapeseed or groundnut oil

300ml/½ pint white wine

1 tablespoon flour

600ml/1 pint fish stock

600ml/1 pint meat stock

bouquet garni

3 lobster shells, smashed up

3 sprigs of tarragon, chopped

lobster butter, to taste (optional, see above)

salt and freshly ground black pepper

Coarsely chop the vegetables and brown them in 2 tablespoons of the oil until just dry, about 20 minutes. Add the wine and reduce most of it away.

In a separate pan, brown the flour in the rest of the oil and add this to the vegetables. Pour in the stocks and bring to the boil. Add the bouquet garni and simmer for about 1 hour. Add the lobster shells and simmer for a further 30 minutes.

Strain, add the chopped tarragon and adjust the seasoning, being generous with the black pepper. Beat in any lobster butter if available.

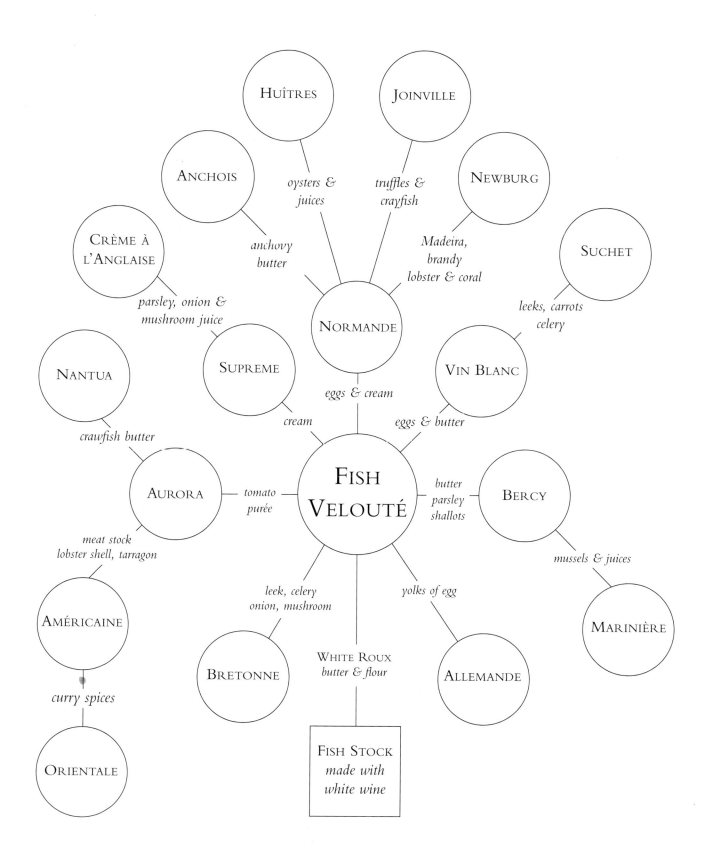

HUÎTRES — oysters & juices

JOINVILLE — truffles & crayfish

ANCHOIS — anchovy butter

NEWBURG — Madeira, brandy lobster & coral

CRÈME À L'ANGLAISE — parsley, onion & mushroom juice

SUCHET — leeks, carrots celery

NORMANDE — eggs & cream

SUPREME — cream

VIN BLANC — eggs & butter

NANTUA — crawfish butter

AURORA — tomato purée

FISH VELOUTÉ

BERCY — butter parsley shallots

MARINIÈRE — mussels & juices

AMÉRICAINE — meat stock lobster shell, tarragon

BRETONNE — leek, celery onion, mushroom

ALLEMANDE — yolks of egg

ORIENTALE — curry spices

WHITE ROUX butter & flour

FISH STOCK made with white wine

## Fish Sauce Family Tree

# Buying, Storing and Preparing Fish & Shellfish

## BUYING

### FRESH FISH

Once you have seen a really fresh fish you will have no worries about being able to distinguish between an old specimen and one that looks as though it may actually still be living and is just lying there waiting to leap away at a touch. The colour is bright, the eye is full and waxy-looking, the body is rigid and sometimes the skin or scales are still covered in a bloom that is tacky to the touch. Even when the fish is washed and gutted it still glistens and is firm. Most importantly it smells only of the sea.

Cutlets and fillets should again be bright and clean, and not be discoloured all over, and flabby, or they are not their best; and if they smell, they will continue to do so when they have been cooked.

### SHELLFISH

Crab and lobster usually have to be ordered ahead if you want to buy them live. (It is advisable to buy them live simply because once dead there is no way of telling how long ago they died!) Otherwise they are sold ready-cooked. Live or cooked, look for ones that are heavy for their size. The tails of cooked lobsters and crayfish should spring back when straightened, showing they were alive when cooked. If loose or flabby, they died some time before.

## PREPARATION

The inside flesh of good, fresh fish needs no rinsing at home, unless it has been dropped on the floor, say. If the gutting has left the cavity soiled or bloody, then the lung cavity may be rinsed clean and wiped carefully with dry paper towels. Filleting should not soil the fish. Slime on the outside may be rinsed off.

### SCALING

The skin of fish can be delicious but the scales are not, so scaling is often necessary. Preferably remove the scales before gutting (ask the fishmonger), but first cut off any dangerous spikes with a pair of scissors before you do it yourself. Then start from the tail end and scrape against the scales up towards the head, paying particular attention to the ridge along the back and around the gills, where they sometimes get overlooked. Do this in the garden or over a newspaper-lined sink and rinse under a tap into a colander to catch the scales, as they block the drain.

### GUTTING

If you are filleting a fish yourself, sometimes you can do it first without gutting the fish (but you obviously then cannot use the bones for stock unless you gut it). Otherwise, insert the knife at the vent and using the tip of the knife slit only the skin open. This avoids the gut and possibly even the flesh from being cut into. Take the knife through the middle of the belly fin bone and up to the head. Change to a pair of scissors and cut through the gut joining the head and then, with your hand, pull away the innards down to the vent, which then needs to be cut free as well. Wipe clean of blood, or rinse.

### SKINNING

Usually only Dover sole, skate and filleted fish are skinned raw (and Dovers are exceptional as the skin can be pulled off slightly diagonally). A not-too-sharp knife is best with fillets. Grasp the tail (with salted fingers to prevent them slipping) and cut through the flesh down to the skin as near to that end as possible. Turn the knife flat and, with the edge towards the head end and pushing and slightly sawing with the knife while wriggling the skin and pulling with the other hand, strip away the skin. This becomes terribly easy after a couple of times.

### FILLETING

This is fun but very time-consuming until you are experienced. However, with care you may get more off your fish than the fishmonger, as he often leaves a lot on the bone (useful if you need bones for stock!).

It is easier to fillet flat fish into four pieces. Remove the head first by cutting around it and through the backbone (which is often tough, so sometimes scissors are easier for an amateur than a knife). Slit through the skin along the backbone from head to tail and, turning the knife flat and using long smooth strokes with a very sharp knife, 'peel' away the flesh from the bone. Do the same with the other pieces.

Cutting flat fish into two fillets is harder. Cut the head off as before, and then insert the tip of the knife flat along the backbone, sharp edge towards the outside edge of the fish and slice it away. Pull the flap of flesh over to expose the backbone and then cut over the backbone and slide the flesh off to the other outside edge to produce one whole side of the fish. Turn it over to do the same on the other side. Check for bones that you have may have cut through and that are left on the fillets.

To fillet round fish, first remove the head by slicing under its fin and round up to the top, and doing the same on the other side. Now twist the head to break the back bone and free it from the body with a pair of scissors. Hold the flesh firm by pressing down flat with one hand. Slit along the back, right down to the tail. Turn the fish over and do the same on the other side. Then cut the flesh away from the bones. Cut through the pin bones (bones that stick out sideways) and take them out with tweezers later. Do the same on the other side.

To fillet skate wings (they should have been skinned by the fishmonger): insert the knife flat in the high bony edge and, slicing with long strokes, roll the flesh back towards the outside edge. Be careful not to break through the skeleton to the other side. Turn over and do the same on the other side.

To prepare John Dory: using scissors cut away the head and the ridged bones all around the fish (beware of the sharp fins). This leaves a neat fish which can be used as it is or filleted, cutting away both sides. It may also now be skinned if necessary.

To prepare monkfish (usually only the tail is sold so preparation is easy): first remove the black–grey mottled skin. Starting at the head end and gripping a piece of this firmly, pull it off cleanly in one piece over the fins and all. Underneath are untidy, fleshy appurtenances that must be sliced off as they shrink on cooking and force the flesh to curl up and distort. Cut away a lot, using the off-cuts for stock. Alternatively, fillet the skinned fish off the very simple backbone (no pin bones here). Laying the piece skinned side down, cut through to the flesh at the bone as if you were skinning a flat fish fillet (above). Using not too sharp a knife, wriggle and push the knife away from you, cutting off unwanted pieces.

## SHELLFISH ETC.

*Mussels* must be scraped clean and any large pieces of the 'beard' (with which it clings to the rocks) pulled away. Later, having cooked the mussels, the remaining beards can be eased off and any pea crabs or pearls removed from inside the fish. Do not soak in water (or feed with oatmeal, etc.) – this is done expertly at mussel cleaning stations.

*Scallops* must on no account be soaked in iced water. If you do that the only method of cooking then available is poaching them in the water they have absorbed. Rinse scallops clean of mud and remove the frill and gristle that is on the main scallops (and use for stock). Retain any orange coral if you like it and discard the feathery brown gill-like piece as well as any black matter. Pat the edible bits dry as soon as possible.

*Clams*, like mussels, may need to be rinsed free of mud before cooking. They are also farmed and so have been cleaned professionally.

There is little preparation with a *lobster*. Usually it is cut in half lengthwise and the stomach and intestines removed. Everything else is edible. There may be bright red coral and some soft, greenish liver (tomalley). There is a nasty spiky bone on the inside of the chest shell that is sometimes pulled off and discarded.

It does not hurt *squid* to be washed well, especially as the tentacles have scaly bits to keep them in shape. Most of these will wash away. Pull the head away from the sack and squeeze above the eyes to find the junction between tentacles and unusable gut. Here is the beak of the fish (mouth), which is pulled away. Then cut across and discard the gut/innards. Pull out the transparent quill from the sac and discard.

Rinse the sac well to clean out the milky residue inside. If you wish to keep the flesh white, peel off the thin outer skin (or leave it and it will tint the flesh an attractive pink when it is cooked). Remove the two fins and reserve (they are tougher but can still be cooked). Slice the sac into strips, rounds or leave whole and cut the tentacles into manageable sizes.

*Acknowledgement*

Sonia Stevenson would like to express her gratitude to Ken Condon of Wandsworth for sharing his boundless knowledge of fish and taking her *twice* to Billingsgate in the small hours.

## GUIDE TO SUPPLIERS

For those without a good local fishmonger, the following is a selection of sources of first-rate fresh fish and other seafood or smoked fish, many of whom will supply by mail order.
ABBOTSBURY OYSTERS, Weymouth, Dorset (Tel 01305 788867 fax 01305 760661)
GEORGE ARMSTRONG, Edinburgh

(Tel 0131 315 2033) *fishmonger and smokehouse*
CONDON FISHMONGERS, London SW8 (Tel 0171 622 2934)
STEVE DOWNEY, Barrow Gurney, nr Bristol (Tel 01275 474707 fax 01275 474708) *fishmonger*
THE DUCHY OF CORNWALL OYSTER FARM, Falmouth (Tel 01326 40210)
THE GALLOWAY SMOKEHOUSE, Newton Stewart, Dumfries &

Galloway (Tel 01671 820354 fax 01671 820545)
STEVE HATT, London N1 (Tel/fax 0171 266 3963) *fishmonger*
THE LLANDUDNO FISH SHOP (Tel 01492 870430 fax 01492 870327)
LOCH FYNE SMOKEHOUSE, Argyll (Tel 01499 600217 fax 01499 600234)
MITCHELL TONKS, Bath fish market (Tel 01225 447794) *fishmonger*

ORKNEY SEAFAYRE, Kirkwall (Tel/fax 01856 761544) *shellfish*
REGENCY FISHERIES, Leamington Spa (Tel 01926 831843)
SEASALTER SHELLFISH, Whitstable, Kent (Tel 01227 272003 fax 01227 264829)
SPINK & SONS, Arbroath (Tel 01241 872023 fax 01241 875663) *Arbroath smokies*
KEN WATMOUGH, Aberdeen (Tel 01224 640321) *fishmonger*